CAREERS in

WRITING

BLYTHE CAMENSON

SECOND EDITION

New York Chicago San Francisco Lisbon London Madrid Mexico City
Milan New Delhi San Juan Seoul Singapore Sydney Toronto

The McGraw·Hill Companies

Library of Congress Cataloging-in-Publication Data

Camenson, Blythe.
     Careers in writing / by Blythe Camenson.—2nd ed.
       p.   cm.
     Includes bibliographical references.
     ISBN 0-07-148212-1 (alk. paper)
     1. Authorship—Vocational guidance.   I. Title.

PN151.C279 2008
808'.02—dc22   2007010576

1 2 3 4 5 6 7 8 9 10 11 12 13 14 15 16 17 18 19 20 21   DOC/DOC   0 9 8 7

ISBN 978-0-07-148212-7
MHID   0-07-148212-1

McGraw-Hill books are available at special quantity discounts to use as premiums and sales promotions, or for use in corporate training programs. For more information, please write to the Director of Special Sales, Professional Publishing, McGraw-Hill, Two Penn Plaza, New York, NY 10121-2298. Or contact your local bookstore.

This book is printed on acid-free paper.

CONTENTS

ACKNOWLEDGMENTS

I would like to thank the following professionals for providing advice and career information:

Linda Addison, Poet

Nancy Bereano, Editor

Marjorie Braman, Executive Editor

Ginger Buchanan, Executive Editor

Joan Camenson, Advertising Copywriter

Kent Carroll, Editor

Suzanne Casey, Freelance Reporter and Stringer

Julie Castiglia, Literary Agent

Jane Chelius, Literary Agent

Rob Cohen, Literary Agent

Jim Cochran, Technical Writer/Producer/Director

Susan Ditz, Public Relations Writer

Elizabeth English, Screenwriter

Paula Eykelhof, Senior Editor

Kathleen Frost, Documentation Specialist

Russell Galen, Literary Agent

Laura Anne Gilman, Author and Editor

Jan Goldberg, Nonfiction Book Writer

Marcus Grimm, Radio Copywriter

Rod Stafford Hagwood, Fashion Writer/Editor

Christina Hamlett, Screenwriter

Joseph Hayes, Freelance Writer

Martha Hollis, Nonfiction Book Writer

Susan Isaacs, Novelist

Barbara Karst-Sabin, Technical Writer

Anne Marie King-Jakubiak, Reporter

Frances Kuffel, Author and Writing Coach

Tanya Lochridge, Freelance Medical/Health-Care Writer

Newman Mallon, Public Relations Writer

Bob Mansker, Former Deputy Public Printer of the United States

Evan Marshall, Literary Agent

Wendy McCurdy, Editor

Linda B. Morelli, Novelist

George Nicholson, Literary Agent

Lori Perkins, Literary Agent

Clay Reynolds, Novelist

Marina Richards, Advertising/Marketing Writer

Karen Taylor Richman, Editor

Pesha Rubenstein, Literary Agent

Peter Rubie, Literary Agent

Anne Savarese, Senior Editor

John Scognamiglio, Senior Editor

Michael Seidman, Editorial Consultant

Judith Smith-Levin, Novelist

Carma Spence-Pothitt, Newsletter Writer

Barbara Stahura, Freelance Writer

Polly Starnes, Media Relations Consultant/Speechwriter

Cherry Weiner, Literary Agent

Nancy Yost, Literary Agent

Susan Zeckendorf, Literary Agent

I also wish to thank Josephine Scanlon for her assistance in preparing this revision.

CHAPTER

1

THE WRITER'S LIFE

"Publication of early work is what a writer needs most of all in life."
—Erskine Caldwell

Although writers come from all sorts of backgrounds and differ from one person to the next, they do have a few things in common. First and foremost, writers love words. They love how they sound and feel and how they fit together in original and rhythmic ways.

Writers love playing with an idea and letting it grow, shaping it into an article, advertisement, story, novel, or nonfiction book.

They love the sense of accomplishment they feel when a project has been completed, when it satisfies a client, or when it finds a home in a book or magazine.

They love seeing their name in print, giving them credit for their writing, and they love receiving the check, which in essence is acknowledgment for a job well done.

Despite all of the highs that writers feel, they face frustrations and disappointments, too. Becoming a professional writer is not an easy task. The new writer faces stiff competition from experienced writers with proven track records. Impersonal rejection slips become a way of life, and novice writers must wonder at times if they have a better shot at winning the lottery than at getting published.

But new writers do get published every year—more often than lottery players win big prizes. It takes a lot of persistence and a little luck, but if it's what you want more than anything else, you can make it happen. Just as you have to buy that ticket in order to win the lottery, if your dream is to become a published writer, you have to keep writing and submitting your work to make it happen.

Some new writers get stalled early on, before their careers even get a chance to take off. They write and write but are reluctant to submit their work. The problem often boils down to fear of rejection—but learning to deal with rejection is a very big part of this exciting career. Although even professional writers are turned down occasionally, savvy writers let rejections guide them rather than hinder them. A rejection means you took the chance and submitted your work for approval—and you should congratulate yourself on taking that huge first step, even if the outcome wasn't what you'd hoped for.

Rejection could also mean that the work you submitted was not right for that particular editor or agent, for that particular publishing house or publication—nothing more, nothing less. Let the rejection encourage you to revise your work or retarget the markets to which you submit it.

As unpleasant as it can be, however, rejection isn't the only adversity that writers face. Self-employed writers work alone and can often feel isolated—until the phone rings, that is, and a friend wants to chat. It can be difficult to convince friends and family that although you work at home, you do indeed have a real job and can't take off work at a moment's notice.

Writers must also cope with irregular paychecks and financial insecurity, at least until they are established. But even then, they can't be sure how often a check will arrive and how many checks there will be each year. (And be prepared for some people to respond to your concerns about finances by telling you to get a "real" job!)

But writing is certainly a real job. Writers facing deadlines often put in more hours than their nine-to-five friends. They work days, nights, weekends, and holidays. They bring the laptop on vacation, working every spare moment they possibly can. Successful writers are disciplined, even driven. They are multitaskers who can set priorities and meet deadlines, whether from an editor or self-imposed. Most feel that writing isn't even a choice; it's something they are compelled to do, just as something compelled you to pick up this book.

In the pages ahead you will learn about all the different writing careers and how you can get started in each one. You'll meet some successful writers and find out how they started and pursued their careers. (Note that though most have college degrees—with majors ranging from math to English to computers—their educational backgrounds aren't featured. For the most part, formal university degree programs don't guide students toward professional writing careers.)

In Appendix A you'll find contact information for professional associations, and in Appendix B a list of useful reference and how-to books. As much as successful writers love to write, they also love to read—and they know that reading about writing is an important part of the process.

C H A P T E R

2

WRITING FICTION

"There are three rules for writing the novel. Unfortunately, no one knows what they are."
—*W. Somerset Maugham*

"Writing a novel is a terrible experience, during which the hair often falls out and the teeth decay."
—*Flannery O'Connor*

To be completely honest, we'll have to admit that the fiction-writing arena is the most difficult area in which to establish your career. It might take quite a while to break in, even to get just one novel published. Markets for short stories have shrunk over the years, and unless you have the talent and good fortune of a Billy Collins or Maya Angelou, chances are you won't be able to make a full-time living as a poet.

If your goal is to see your name not only on a book jacket but also among the top ten on bestseller lists, remember there are only a few slots and millions of writers who share your aspirations.

Having said that, with writing ability—or the willingness to work hard and learn your craft—an understanding of how the marketplace works, and a great deal of persistence, getting your fiction published is not impossible. A lucky few might even make it big. Stephen King had to start somewhere. His first novel, *Carrie*, was rejected dozens of times before it found a home. Let's look at what's involved.

FIVE STEPS TO CREATING A SALABLE PRODUCT

As in any industry, if you are going to sell something, you must have a quality product the public wants to buy. How you go about creating that product will, in part, determine how successful you'll be.

To create a marketable product, in this case a salable manuscript, you need to follow five steps. Although they may seem obvious, many new writers ignore them. But as you read on, you'll see how much weight publishing professionals put on these factors.

Step 1: Read Before You Write

Before you begin to write, agents and editors will advise you to read other writers. Study their style, content, and technique. Use your reading to gain an understanding of the marketplace and to determine if what you want to write will fit in.

"The best advice I can give," says agent Nancy Yost of Lowenstein-Yost Associates, a New York–based literary agency, "is read, read, and read some more. It's important to read other writers and to know what other people are reading. The best writers are avid readers."

Reading other people's work will give you a more in-depth understanding of the marketplace, and it will help you to improve your own writing as well.

Editor Kent Carroll, founder of Europa Editions, says, "Take a book you like and go through it a second time. Dissect it, take it apart to see how the thing is structured, what the convention of storytelling is. Pay particular attention to how the book is organized. I think you can learn a lot from that. But don't just imitate it. Let it come from your own heart, your own mind, your own imagination."

"Read a lot, but not just the established writers, such as Danielle Steel or Stephen King," advises agent Pesha Rubenstein. "Read everything current, the new authors that are being put out now. This is the kind of material that publishers are looking for."

Karen Taylor Richman, an editor at Silhouette, gives the same advice. "*Read! Read! Read!* The one thing an author and editor have in common is their love for words. Knowing your market, understanding where you're sending your manuscript and why you feel a certain house is the one for your book, is probably the most important homework a person can do.

Remember, everything you're seeing out on the shelves now was bought a while ago, so something you are sure is a new idea or a fresh twist may not be. The key is to be professional about it. And if you want to write for Silhouette, you should be reading Silhouette books to get a feel for what we're looking for."

Editorial consultant Michael Seidman advises, "Read fiction, all kinds of fiction. I've found that reading bestsellers is a frustrating experience, because no one can tell you why a particular book made it in spite of everything that's wrong with it. But, if nothing else, it will reaffirm for you the fact that sometimes God smiles, and why shouldn't that smile grace you?"

Marjorie Braman, vice president and executive editor at HarperCollins, sums it up nicely. "If you want to be a writer, the best thing you can do for yourself, for a number of reasons, is to read a lot. There's the commercial reason of knowing what's working and how to tailor your book for a specific audience. And also, if you read voraciously, it opens you up to a broader approach in your own writing. You can hone your skills by reading people who are good writers."

Some writers say they don't read other authors because they fear their own work might be negatively affected. Don't fall into this mind-set, which can sabotage new writers. Nancy Bereano, founder of Firebrand Books, says, "When writers say to me, 'Oh, I never read anyone else because I don't want to be influenced by them,' I laugh hysterically. Give me a break."

Step 2: Write for the Market

Editors and agents are on your side. They want you to be aware of the market and to write for it—after all, without commercial product, they would have nothing to sell.

Many new writers try to write without knowing the market, and don't think about selling their book until it is complete. Remember that you've got to write to the market—if you are writing a romance, you have to understand romance novels; if you are writing science fiction, you have to have a good idea of what is already on the shelves and what people are buying. And if you want to have your book considered by a particular publisher, become familiar with that publisher's list.

"Remember, you need to sell yourself to an agent or an editor, and you won't have a lot of success if you are just stumbling around in a vacuum," says Ginger Buchanan, executive editor of Penguin's Ace Books. "Read *Publishers Weekly*. Read magazines on the genre you are interested in. Study the markets so you know what is happening. It's basic, but you won't get anywhere without paying attention to those types of details. Later, you can rely on your agent to keep track of markets and trends, but beginning writers really have to know what the business is doing. If you don't work hard at the business end of your writing, you're just dooming yourself to disappointment."

Peter Rubie, founder of the Peter Rubie Literary Agency, says, "I'm not out there to say no, although people have that impression about agents. But the reality is that the bulk of material agents receive is just not up to a publishable standard. I love to come across great material, but people don't read enough and have no idea what's fresh and what isn't, what's been done or what hasn't."

Step 3: Write for Yourself

Although Step 3 sounds as if it contradicts the advice in Step 2, it really doesn't. Writing for the market and writing for yourself can coexist. Market-savvy writers understand the fine line here and know how to blend both elements.

Agent Russell Galen of Scovil, Chichak, Galen Literary Agency, Inc., has this to say: "The writing process should be shaped internally, by the writer himself, not by me or by the marketplace. It isn't simply that this makes for better books, though of course it does; it actually makes for more commercial books. When the writing process is shaped externally, the result is always an obvious knockoff, an ersatz Rolex made in Hong Kong, and I can spot it."

"Write what you love to read," says agent Cherry Weiner of the Cherry Weiner Literary Agency. "All too often writers will say that they really love such and such a genre, but they will never get in, so they are going to write something else because it's easier. Nothing is easy to write. If you don't love the genre you are writing in, it will show and you won't make it."

"I think writers should write what they like," says John Scognamiglio, senior editor at Kensington Books. "I don't think a writer should decide to write a historical romance just because that's what's selling now. They need to combine what they like to read or write with what's selling."

Anne Savarese, senior editor at Princeton University Press, says, "It's easier to sell a first novel if it fits into some kind of genre. But often writers worry too much about tailoring their work to what they think publishers want. Even to the point of what kind of novel they're going to write. I think it's best to be true to what you want to do. If you have a novel in mind, you should write that novel as well as you can. Certainly you want to send it to a publisher who will most likely be interested in it, but sometimes, for example, new writers will say, 'Oh, these techno-thrillers are really big, why don't I write one of those?' But that's usually not a good idea. If you're not writing something you're really interested in, or know well, it's going to show."

Paula Eykelhof, senior editor at Harlequin Superromance, says, "Write the story that's close to your heart. Are you drawn to stories of strong, risk-taking women, stories with adventure, stories that feature family drama? Write what you want to read—and do it in your own way."

Jane Chelius of the Jane Chelius Literary Agency says, "Don't worry about the market, where you think the market is, where you think the market is going. The market is very, very tough. I think you have to write your own book. You might as well write the book that's your heart's desire, because it's too hard to psych out the market. You know, we're seeing some very unusual, quirky things work really well."

"Don't try to fake it," advises Evan Marshall, president of the Evan Marshall Agency. "Write only the kind of books you love to read and never deviate from that. Find your niche and stay in it and believe in yourself. Don't leave it just because you get rejected. If you're really good, you will be published."

Step 4: Learn How to Write

This seems like such an obvious step, you might be wondering why it's even included. But it's a step too many new writers overlook. You might have been reading avidly all your life, perhaps even saying to yourself, "I could do a much better job than this," and feel more than ready to begin writing. And yes, reading other writers does help with your own writing. But it's often not enough to bring your work up to publishable standards.

Let's compare an aspiring writer with an aspiring physician. It's true that part of the training for a medical student is to observe seasoned doctors at work. But before a student is even allowed in a hospital room or an operating theater, he or she must attend lectures, read and absorb count-less textbooks, and study, study, study. Can you imagine a med student being shown on the first day an operating table with a tray of instruments next to it—and being told to begin a surgical procedure? Hardly. Learning how to write is not something that happens in a day or in a vacuum either. Yes, being an avid reader is an important part of the process, but it is an ongoing process, and there are other elements to consider.

Here are some avenues to pursue to learn the craft of writing.

How-To Books. In addition to your mainstream or genre reading, don't forget the textbooks of the trade. Hundreds of how-to books for writers are available on every aspect of writing the novel. They cover writing in general and narrow in on specific topics. Want more insight into plot, dia-logue, characterization, voice, style, viewpoint, action, and conflict? A book out there covers it.

You can find books on grammar, too. You've probably heard about this or that famous writer who couldn't spell or whose grammar was atrocious. Wouldn't an editor fix those problems? Maybe at one time, but in today's market that writer would have a difficult time getting work considered seri-ously, never mind published. Of course, an agent or editor would be will-ing to work with a writer whose talent outweighed the errors, but the story and characters would have to be pretty outstanding to hold someone's attention beyond the first paragraph.

Magazines and Newsletters. In addition to how-to books, there are very good periodicals to help you. *Writer's Digest* magazine, *The Writer*, and countless newsletters put out by various writers associations are all good sources of useful information.

University Writing Programs. Many new writers pursue a master's degree in writing, and for some this is an excellent way to sharpen their skills. But professionals—authors, agents, and editors—have mixed feelings about these programs. Editorial consultant Michael Seidman says, "I think they can be brilliant training grounds, but too many of them are insular and wind up teaching you how to teach a master's course. But, they can serve to stretch your imagination and force you to look at writing from perspec-tives that might not be your usual ones. So, in the end, if you have the time and finances to attend, I'd go for it."

Bestselling author Susan Isaacs is glad she didn't attend a writing program. "If I had taken a writing class, I would surely have lost [my own writing voice] and come out writing present-tense fiction like everyone else in New York."

Adult Education Programs. Rather than committing to a full-scale graduate program, many beginning writers choose to take courses at adult education programs offered by local two- and four-year colleges. Many such programs offer workshops, seminars, and classes taught by solid, experienced writers and teachers.

Writers' Conferences. Writers' conferences are another good vehicle for improving your skills. They are excellent for networking and meeting agents, editors, and other writers, and they also afford you the opportunity to hear successful authors speak on novel-writing techniques.

Julie Castiglia, founder of Castiglia Literary Agency, agrees that a new writer must invest some time, money, and energy in learning the craft. "People just have an idea or write a book out of nowhere and then look for an agent. They think they can tackle a book without spending any money or effort on training. They expect their book to be top-notch without going to writers' conferences, taking classes, or learning the craft of writing. Even if you are very talented, you need instruction and networking in order to develop your writing to the fullest potential. If you haven't invested yourself in learning to write, you are wasting your time seeking an agent."

Writers' conferences are beneficial for starting writers, especially in some of the genre areas. Romance, mystery, and science fiction have many writers' conferences, and they are useful not only for educational purposes but also for moral support. They give you a sense that you are not alone.

Support Groups. Many writers rely on critique or support groups, knowing that a well-chosen group with a particular focus and a set of guidelines to follow can provide valuable feedback on their work.

Editor John Scognamiglio says, "You should always try to get someone to read your work. A lot of times writers can't distance themselves enough, and someone else might find something you might have missed. Some writers belong to a critique group or have a writing partner. A writer shouldn't be afraid of criticism; part of writing is rejection. It's just a matter of building a tough shell and knowing what your strengths and weaknesses are."

Agent George Nicholson of Sterling Lord Literistic says, "I think it is important to belong to a writers group, but it is also important to be your own person. Too many novice writers are uncertain about their skills and pay too much attention to what others say. While it is important to listen to what others say, trust in your own instincts and judgment."

Critiques. Paid critiquing by a trusted professional is another possibility to consider. The critic's comments can help pinpoint your problem areas and offer suggestions on how to correct them.

Think back to our earlier example of doctors learning their profession. Considering the investment of both time and money that a doctor has to make to pursue a medical career, writers have it easy. A few how-to books, some market guides, a well-chosen conference or two a year, perhaps a manuscript critique, all add up to a small amount of money, comparatively speaking, and it is money well spent.

As agent Evan Marshall says, "Before you even approach an agent, learn your market inside out and master the techniques of your craft the best you can."

Step 5: Polish Your Product

Many new writers are so excited about the prospect of seeing their name in print that they rush too quickly to place their material in the hands of agents and acquisitions editors. Typing "The End" on that last page isn't necessarily your signal to get the mailers and SASEs (self-addressed, stamped envelopes) ready.

Of course completing your novel is cause for celebration. Many people will tell you they have a great book in them, but only a small percentage actually sit down and write that book. You're one of a select few who have devoted themselves to producing a finished product. But is it really finished? In the rush to publish, many new writers inadvertently defeat their own efforts. They send out their first draft instead of their tenth; sloppily prepared manuscripts; novels with grammatical errors and typos; or short stories with point of view problems, plotting problems, characterization problems, and loose ends galore.

"I really believe in writers rewriting their material," says editor John Scognamiglio. "When someone sends something off it should be really polished. Writers learn a lot when they go over their material. I think you can get better if you keep working at it."

Agents and editors receive countless submissions, most of which are rejected. Some submissions are inappropriate—they have been mistargeted, sent to the wrong house or agency. Others exhibit amateur writing or offer tired story lines. Editors and agents can easily spot first-novel problems. If you learn how to spot those problems in your own work before sending it out, you'll be giving yourself an edge against the competition.

FIRST-NOVEL PROBLEMS

Listen to what the experts say. Here several agents and editors comment on what they consider to be deal-breakers, sure guarantees of a rejection letter finding its way into your mailbox.

Plot

Evan Marshall, agent, Evan Marshall Literary Agency. "I get novels where it looks as if someone just sat down and started typing without any overall plan—didn't think about who would be the best viewpoint character, for example. I've seen every possible kind of craziness: books told completely in summary, novels all in narration or all in dialogue.

"Not paying attention to plot is like saying you want to paint, but you don't know how to open the tubes. Plot is not just a series of events worming their way around. Everything has to grow organically from what happened before it."

The Hook

Marjorie Braman, vice president and executive editor, HarperCollins. "Often new writers don't understand how important the first part of the book is. The success of the first half of the book is, in some ways, more important than the success of the second half of the book. The opening scene is especially important. It's not the place to establish plot or setting. The first scene or the first chapter is the place to draw readers in and get them hooked. There are a number of different ways to do it, but too often I see too much effort going into setting up the book in the first chapter. That's not what a first chapter is for."

Wendy McCurdy, editor, Bantam Books. "It can't just be another formula story, no matter how well done. That's just not going to be good enough. I am looking for something with a real hook, something for which I can visualize the niche it's going to reach."

Ginger Buchanan, executive editor, Ace Books. "By far the biggest problem I encounter when reading manuscripts by new writers is a thinness of imagination. I receive plenty of perfectly well-written books that have nothing original to say, because the writers read only books that are exactly like the ones they are trying to write."

Pace

Russell Galen, agent, Scovil, Chichak, Galen Literary Agency, Inc. "Timing, pacing, rhythm. Inexperienced writers often neglect to put themselves in the reader's shoes and envision for themselves what the reading experience will be like, and as a result, their books are often paced in a way that isn't as enjoyable for the reader as it should be. Most commonly, this shows itself in pacing that is too slow, scenes that drag on, revelations that take forever to come, and when they finally come, it's too late and we've lost patience and interest.

"New writers often have trouble balancing all the different elements of the story. It has to move along at a pace the reader won't lose patience with. Sometimes I get the sense that the writer is having such a good time creating the set-up, he forgets about the book as a whole."

Narrative Tension

Susan Zeckendorf, agent, Susan Zeckendorf Associates, Inc. "Another problem, which is especially true of mysteries and thrillers, is that there isn't enough suspense or narrative tension. There needs to be something to make the reader want to keep turning the pages."

Anne Savarese, senior editor, Princeton University Press. "Often books can be very well written, but they are just not compelling enough. A lot of books we see are competent but not so good we think we have to publish them. Those are more problematic: There's no one thing that's specifically wrong. It just doesn't raise the temperature of the editor who's reading it to make him or her take the next step. And it's harder to really define why that happens. It just doesn't grab you, or it grabs you a little but not enough, or it seems derivative, just like ten other novels you've read that year. The mark of skillful writers is that their work stands out."

Storytelling

Laura Anne Gilman, author and editor, DYMK Productions, Writing, and Editorial Services. "A writer may have a good story and may write well but won't know how to tell the story. Sometimes the story isn't developed properly. There may be only 70,000 to 80,000 words written, but the story could be expanded to develop it better. Or the opposite can happen, that too much is told. A writer may put everything in from the research, while only some of it is needed for flavor and accuracy."

Michael Seidman, consultant, Michael Seidman Editorial Consultations. "A good book is a combination of factors, all of which lead back to the same point—storytelling. If a writer is aware that storytelling is an extension of an oral tradition, if there's a distinctive voice, if something's happening that makes a difference in the reader's life, if there are characters you can believe in and care about who speak the way people speak, that's all that counts."

Peter Rubie, agent, Peter Rubie Literary Agency. "A lot of people come up with a good idea, but they don't know how to tell the story. But you could take a fairly mundane idea and if you tell it well enough, you can probably get it published."

Characters

Marjorie Braman. "Any time I like a character immediately or want to know more about him or her, then the author has done the job of at least attracting my attention. I'm always drawn in by character and less by plot. As an editor, plot is something I can help with suggestions about, but character and the emotional content of a book are something I can't teach. It's something that's either natural or not, so if authors have that, they've won a big battle."

Susan Zeckendorf. "Sometimes characters are not particularly original or well-developed. They should be described, not just in narrative but through their actions and dialogue. And if too many characters are introduced up front, it's difficult to remember who they all are."

Rob Cohen, agent, The Cohen Agency. "If I have a wonderful character, other shortcomings are less important to me. For a lot of agents, though, it's the writing or the actual plot. What kind of character do I find exciting? One that is unique, unusual, or just a lot of fun, and one that I can identify with."

Nancy Love, agent, The Nancy Love Literary Agency. "The thing that hooks me right off in a novel is the characters. Characters are the beginning of a book. If I don't care about the characters, I will reject it right away."

Dialogue

Evan Marshall. "Dialogue is another trouble spot. It's stiff and unrealistic or it doesn't get us anywhere. Dialogue should pretend that it's imitating life, but it doesn't really. It isn't supposed to have the incidental inconsequentials we say everyday like 'Hi, how are you?'"

Marjorie Braman. "I think that dialogue can be difficult, and in order to write realistic dialogue, you have to have a good ear. All you really have to do, of course, is listen to people around you—to strangers, to friends, and to family. But somehow, when it gets put down on paper, especially by a first-time novelist, it tends to turn rather unrealistic. An ear for good dialogue is something I think must come with time, but it should be paid attention to."

Cherry Weiner. "Often I see authors who are 'aspiring toward literary.' In effect, what happens is that the dialogue is stilted and formal. It doesn't sound like natural, everyday language."

The Writing Style

Evan Marshall. "The texture of the writing itself is often a problem, using too many adjectives and adverbs or giving every line of dialogue a tag with an adverb attached. That's amateurish. You can tell they're either not reading the books that explain what good writing is or they're not absorbing the information.

"Editors are fussier than ever, and so often I get fiction that is untrained as far as the technical aspects—viewpoint, dialogue, writing style, the misuse of adjectives and adverbs, whatever constitutes good writing as opposed to bad writing."

Laura Anne Gilman. "Good writing gets me excited. The story can be mediocre, but if you can write, I will give you the story back and tell you to send me another story. Good writing will overcome just about anything.

"Expository lumps are a turnoff! It's more than just going on and on without saying anything. It's writing for the sake of the words when there is no action. If you are reading and your eyes glaze over, or you begin skipping lines, that's an expository lump."

Nancy Love. "A lot of the novels I see need much more tightening up. The writer sends it out too soon. The manuscript could benefit from a workshop or critique group."

Content

Evan Marshall. "A lot of the books I get are about things that aren't of interest anymore—or never were. This has to do with awareness of market. For example, there are really very few KGB/CIA thrillers published anymore, but I still receive tons of them. Or books about an AIDS-like virus that's decimating the country, and some brave heroine is going to find out what laboratory is doing this. Or novels of historical fiction without a romance element set in some obscure time period in some obscure place with little interest to anyone. And no one's publishing multigenerational sagas unless you're a big name. The writer is confusing fresh ideas with out-of-the-market ideas. First be within the market and then be fresh."

Frances Kuffel, author and writing coach, former agent, Jean Naggar Literary Agency. "Too many first novels often tend to be coming-of-age novels, autobiographical in nature, about that person's experiences growing up. But the coming-of-age novel is extremely difficult to sell at this time. Several years ago the coming-of-age novel was hot. It just isn't anymore."

Voice

Marjorie Braman. "If a book is written in a voice that I don't like, that's a turnoff. For example, I'm not very fond of a humorous voice in mysteries, or one that tries too hard to be humorous.

"And an author who stands on a soapbox in a novel turns me off. Certainly, there are ways to get your point across and be entertaining at the same time, but if I feel I'm being preached to, I don't feel I'm being entertained. In fiction, the first goal is to entertain."

Viewpoint

Evan Marshall. "I advise new writers to avoid using the first person. It smacks of first novel or of gothic, and first person is difficult to sell. Some editors just don't like it. When you're just starting out, you want everything going in your favor. Why turn off three out of ten editors because of the viewpoint you've chosen?

"But the place to start thinking about this is before you begin writing. You have to decide who your viewpoint characters will be, from whose point of view the story will be told. A lot of authors don't understand the concept. That includes everything from knowing how to keep to one viewpoint in a scene, all the way to deciding who's going to be your viewpoint character.

"A multiple third-person point of view [telling the story from several main characters' points of view] is right for a bigger book with a more ambitious plot. You decide on four or five main viewpoint characters and stick to them, and you do each scene using just one of those viewpoints. You don't change viewpoints in the middle of a scene; editors shriek and grimace when they see it.

"For a smaller book, especially in certain genres, sometimes one viewpoint character is right, such as in a woman-in-jeopardy or a mystery. Use only one character's viewpoint and tell it in third person."

Background Details

Russell Galen. "Many books begin with long expositions of background, postponing until deep in the book any clear reason to keep reading. It's almost as common for a book to rush on too fast, not slowing down to lay in the necessary rich detail and background that enables characters to come alive."

Pesha Rubenstein, agent, Pesha Rubenstein Literary Agency Inc. "A new writer often tries to present life exactly as it is, such as telling me every minute of the day or overdoing the dialogue. Things have to be true to life, but it can't be verbatim. Linear writing is also a problem. It's not necessary to chronicle every minute of every day in sequence. You need to jump right into the action."

Laura Anne Gilman. "Either the writer will throw in too much background material to tell what happened in the beginning, or omit so much it leaves the reader guessing. A balance has to be made, and that is difficult to do. It's not uncommon for writers to have problems with this on their second or third novels as well."

Grammar

Lori Perkins, agent, L. Perkins Agency. "Clean up your grammar! It's not that most people can't write, but often new writers have terrible grammar, spelling, and punctuation. Study it and give me a high-quality manuscript."

Word Count

Laura Anne Gilman. "We use word count rather than page length because printers can vary so. A novel should be somewhere between 75,000 words and 100,000 words. Anything shorter than that isn't a novel. Longer than, say, 120,000 words is what we call a 'fat book' and becomes extremely hard to sell because the cost of printing it is so high. Mostly that length is reserved for the established or the breakout authors." (A breakout author sells much better than the publisher had anticipated, becoming a surprise bestseller. An example would be Gregory Maguire's novel *Wicked,* which caught on right after its publication, selling an estimated four hundred thousand copies even before plans for the musical version were announced.)

Frances Kuffel. "Keep it short. I have a novel right now that's pretty good, but it's six hundred pages long. That will never sell because of the publisher's cost for actually producing the work. People should be thinking, 'How can I make this shorter? How can I make it tighter?'"

SIX STEPS TO GETTING PUBLISHED

New writers learn soon enough that writing a novel is only half the battle. The other half is getting it published. How you target your submissions and how you approach editors or agents carry equal weight when producing a salable product.

Here's a step-by-step program that will help you sell your product.

Step 1: Target Your Submissions

Do your homework. Don't send a romance novel to a sci-fi publisher. Don't send a children's picture book to an agent who handles only adult fiction. Study the market guides (see Appendix B), attend conferences and meet with editors and agents face to face, talk to other writers, join professional associations geared to helping writers learn the ropes (see Appendix A).

Step 2: Craft Your Query Letter

The query letter is your first introduction to editors and agents. It's a miniproposal, with the purpose of hooking agents or editors and getting them to ask to see more. The query letter should be one page only, show-case your best writing, and avoid the mistakes many new writers make (going into too much detail, not giving enough specifics, using book-review-style copy to describe your work—save the book reviews for the book reviewers—and predicting bestseller status). Sample query letters are provided for you later in this chapter. (See Figures 2.1 and 2.2.)

Step 3: Send Them What They Want

A successful query letter will produce requests for more. The agents or editors will tell you what to send—sample chapters or the full manuscript, and possibly a synopsis. Check the agent's or publisher's submission guide-lines for authors. Make sure to enclose an SASE—self-addressed, stamped envelope—if one is requested. Pay attention to whether you should submit by mail, fax, or e-mail. If they ask to see sample chapters, send the first few chapters, not chapters selected randomly. And if they ask to see only sample chapters, don't be tempted to send them the entire manuscript anyway.

Step 4: Craft the Synopsis

The most successful synopses are one page, written in present tense, with your main character and his or her conflict as the focus. It's a summary of your novel's plot, written in the same style as the novel. The synopsis should feature your important plot points, but it need not cover every detail or subplot. For resources to help you learn more about writing the synopsis, see Appendix B.

Step 5: Submit a Professional Package

Follow these format rules when submitting your manuscript. Manuscripts should be double-spaced; query letters and synopses should be single-spaced. Right margins should not be justified. Your name, book title, and page number should be in a heading on the top of every page. You should use only white paper, with text printed on one side. Font size should be 12 with black ink in either Times New Roman or Courier. A cover page should include your name, address, phone number, e-mail address, genre, and word count. (But not the copyright symbol. It's a sign you're an amateur if you do include it.) For resources on manuscript format and the submission package, see Appendix B.

Step 6: The Wait

Many new writers send off their material, and then begin the wait. But it can take weeks and, more often than not, months to receive a reply. And, in many cases, the reply will be a rejection. What's the best way to deal with this? Don't wait. Get busy writing your next novel, and the one after that. It's rare for a first novel to break in. If you're hard at work on your next project, rejections on your first won't feel as bad. The more manuscripts you have polished, the more hope you have. Rejection is the name of the game, and successful writers develop a thick skin to cope with it.

SAMPLE QUERY LETTERS

The query letter in Figure 2.1 landed the author an agent. The book subsequently was optioned for a TV movie.

Linda B. Morelli sent her query for *Fiery Surrender* (see Figure 2.2) to nineteen agents. Below is a breakdown of agent responses:

- Four agents were not taking on new clients.
- Six agents were not interested.
- Nine agents requested her synopsis/sample chapters and/or the complete manuscript.

Linda sent her material to the nine who requested more. Here are the responses of those nine:

- Three reported they were not taking on new clients.
- Four felt the book was not for them.
- One was on the West Coast and felt Linda would be better served by a New York agent, since they are close geographically.
- One wrote back a week after receiving her manuscript and asked to represent her.

(On letterhead with your phone number and e-mail address.)

Date

Editor's or Agent's Name, Title (The title isn't necessary for agents.)
Publishing House/Agency
Address

Dear Mr./Ms. Name,

Have you ever been in a new town, then thought you recognized someone from back home? It happens to all of us, imagining a familiar face in a strange environment. But when Abby Clark Trenton started seeing a Matthew Bowman look-alike everywhere she turned, it wasn't a comforting experience. San Angelo, a small coastal community in central California, was the last place she expected to find her first husband. Matthew had been killed aboard Abby's cabin cruiser the year before. He was dead, Abby was sure of it. She ought to know. She had killed him herself.

Widow is a 79,000-word woman-in-jeopardy novel that tells the story of Abby Clark Trenton, a freelance photographer who escapes an abusive marriage and tries to start her life over. She has a new job, a new husband, and a beautiful new home overlooking the ocean.

But now her worst nightmare is here, stalking her, his features slightly altered, denying his identity. Calling himself Ted Lawson, he strikes up a friendship with Abby's new husband, writer Dale Trenton, and installs himself into the Trenton household. It's a friendship Abby is sure will end in tragedy. Too may secrets and too many lies have made it impossible for Abby to confide in Dale fully. She feels powerless to stop the erosion—until she realizes what she must do.

To save herself, her husband, and her marriage, Abby must act first.

She must kill Matthew Bowman . . . yet another time.

I am a full-time writer (four dozen books to my credit) and director of Fiction Writer's Connection, a membership organization for new writers. My bio is attached.

May I send you the complete manuscript?

Sincerely,

Blythe Camenson

Before signing with this agent, Linda checked with Romance Writers of America to ensure he had no complaints against him, spoke with him on the phone, then signed with him.

In spite of her precautions, however, Linda later learned through more networking and her own experiences that the agent/client relationship was not the best fit. She switched to another agent, Linda Hyatt of Hyatt Literary Agency, whom she met at a writers retreat, and she is now happily represented.

Figure 2.2: Sample Query Letter

Date

Agent's Name
Agency Address

Dear Agent's Name,

My historical romance, *Fiery Surrender*, tells the story of Monique von Strade, the headstrong daughter of a Prussian Count who knows from the moment she meets the enigmatic Pierre Latier that he will steal her heart as surely as he will save her honor. But love is the furthest thing from Pierre's mind. He's a man with a dark past who, under the guise of Pierre Marchant, serves King Louis VI as a spy. Pierre can ill afford to think of anything, save his upcoming mission, escorting French arms to the American Colonies.

When Pierre pays a sudden visit to her in Paris, Monique realizes the depth of the love she holds for him. Confessing her unwilling betrothal to a Comte she despises, she agrees to meet Pierre secretly. Within Pierre's passionate embrace, Monique can no longer deny the fierce, burning desires that flood her. Later, believing Pierre married her only to protect her family's honor, she resolves to win his love, even though it means following Pierre into the dangers of war.

Set against the American Revolution and the October 1781 Battle of Yorktown, Virginia, *Fiery Surrender* is a sensual story of two people who eventually face the inevitability of their love. The novel runs approximately 130,000 words and is ready for an agent's assessment. To give authenticity to my novel, I have conducted considerable research at the Library of Congress and in both Williamsburg and Yorktown, Virginia.

I have an extensive background as an editor–creative writer and am an avid reader of historical and contemporary romances. I am an active member of Washington Romance Writers, Virginia Romance Writers, and Romance Writers of America. I am currently in the final stages of completing a second novel, a category mystery romance.

If the premise of the book appeals to you, I'd be happy to send the complete manuscript.

Sincerely yours,

Linda B. Morelli

Linda ultimately edited her manuscript down to ninety thousand words, and *Fiery Surrender* was published by Port Town Publishing.

DO YOU NEED AN AGENT?

Many writers who have submitted their work directly to publishers have gotten published. Some genre publishers, such as romance and mystery, are more than happy to look at submissions sent without an agent. But the majority of the big publishers in New York won't touch a manuscript that comes directly from the writer. A novel that comes from an agent has been screened and deemed at least ready for submission. And many editors feel more comfortable keeping finances out of their relationship with writers.

Agents have an inroad to what publishers are looking for, and good agents rarely mistarget their submissions. Having an agent gives you credibility as a writer and saves you from devoting all your time to marketing your work. With a good agent in your corner, you can spend your time writing and know that your agent will handle the marketing and the money end of the business for you.

Although finding an agent is not easy, it is by no means impossible. A good query letter and an excellent novel will readily attract an agent's attention. If an agent feels he or she can sell your work, there is no reason not to take you on—whether you're new at the game or a veteran author.

The approach you should use for an agent is the same six-step process covered earlier in this chapter. It's not a good idea to target agents and editors at the same time, though. If you have sent your manuscript out to a dozen publishers on your own, then manage to land an agent, there will be no one left for the agent to submit to. If you are unable to find an agent, you might try targeting some of the smaller publishers directly. But first ask yourself why you aren't finding an agent. Is your query letter not sufficiently compelling? Is your manuscript not professionally crafted? Paying attention to these aspects will almost assure you an agent. Resources for finding an agent are found in Appendixes A and B.

No Agent Is Better than a Bad Agent

As in any industry, writers will find that there are unscrupulous people out there, ready to prey on their desperate desire to become published. They'll promise the world, but for a fee, and they don't deliver.

Smart writers know that legitimate agents charge their 15 percent commission only when they sell your work to a publisher. There are no reading fees, evaluation fees, or editing fees. Legitimate agents won't refer you to a book doctor with the promise of representation after you've dished out thousands of dollars and have rewritten your manuscript.

Spotting a Good Agent

When looking for an agent, consider only those who are members of the Association of Authors' Representatives (AAR) (see Appendix A). AAR agents must follow a canon of ethics and are forbidden to charge fees. Agents earn their money by selling your work to publishers, not by collecting from you. You are not responsible for an agent's overhead, or cost of doing business, and don't be convinced otherwise.

Fee chargers are not the only kind of "bad" agents out there. Most "good" agents are in New York City. While many legitimate agents work successfully outside that arena and prejudices over out-of-town agents are dissipating, still, editors want to work with agents who have a proven track record. Do not be afraid to ask prospective agents who they represent and how many sales they have made.

You can expect your agent to communicate with you, to send you editors' responses to your work, to negotiate the best deal for you in case of an acceptance, and to be in your corner as a truthful, hardworking advocate. If this isn't happening, it might be time to move on.

You shouldn't expect your agent to work miracles for you, though. It could take an agent a year or even longer to place your manuscript. If it's been only a few months and no good word has come your way, don't assume it's the agent's fault. Although you can check in with your agent occasionally, don't make frequent phone calls, expecting long conversations and hand-holding. If you keep agents on the phone too much, they won't be able to do their job—selling your manuscript.

WRITING SHORT STORIES AND POETRY

As mentioned at the beginning of this chapter, making a career writing short stories and poetry is next to impossible. Yes, you can get your work published, see your byline, and maybe even receive a small check for your efforts, but the money involved wouldn't be enough to live on.

New writers often wonder if they should start with short stories as a way of breaking into the novel market. Certainly having fiction credits can help show an agent or editor that you're a professional, but each novel you submit stands on its own and is judged by its own merits. Your short story in *Reader's Digest* or *Playboy*, although wonderful clips to have, is not a guarantee of success with novels.

If writing short stories or poetry is what you love to do, then by all means go for it. But as far as making a career of it, well, there's an expression in the writing world that applies here: Don't give up your day job just yet.

POTENTIAL EARNINGS

Some new writers think that novel writing will make them rich and famous. But there are only ten to twelve slots on the bestseller lists, and most of those are taken up by well-known authors. In truth, the average advance for a first novel is in the $5,000 range. Those huge million-dollar deals you hear about are not the norm. Midlist authors can make a comfortable living turning out two or three books a year, but the largest group earns less than a family would need to survive.

In most cases a writer is given an advance check upon acceptance of the manuscript—half at the onset, the other half after any required revisions are turned in. Then a royalty percentage is offered, sometimes based on the retail price of the book, sometimes on the net price. The royalty percentage might start at 6 or 8 percent, then increase with the number of copies that are sold. To receive a royalty check, though, the book first needs to earn back its advance. And sometimes that can take a while.

With short stories and poetry, earnings can be negligible. Smaller magazines might offer just a few dollars or even just complimentary copies of the issue in which your work appears. Some of the more well-known markets, such as *The New Yorker* or *Atlantic Monthly*, pay much higher rates—one or two dollars per word—but these markets are very difficult to break into.

As with any self-employment, as a writer you must take care of your own taxes, health insurance, and any other benefits received by full-time workers.

The more you produce, the more you can earn. But remember, the time you spend marketing your work will equal, if not exceed, the amount of time you spend writing.

Writing fiction is not an easy way to earn money, but if it's what you love to do, don't let financial fears stop you. The next bestseller could be yours, but you'll never know if you don't try.

FIRSTHAND ACCOUNTS

Read the following accounts from three professional fiction writers to see whether you have what it takes to pursue this dream career.

JUDITH SMITH-LEVIN
Mystery Writer

Judith Smith-Levin is the author of the Starletta Duvall mystery series. The first book, *Do Not Go Gently*, was published by HarperCollins in 1995. The next three books, *The Hoodoo Man*, *Green Money*, and *Reckless Eyeballin'*, have all been published by Random House.

In addition to novels, Judith's writing experience includes journalism, television news writing, teleplays, film scripts, and theatrical plays. She also teaches courses in novel writing.

The Attraction to Writing

Judith says that she has been reading since age three and has always loved words and the beauty of language. Because writing came naturally, she dreamed of being published as a novelist. She didn't plan on writing mystery novels, however; that sort of snuck up on her.

Judith owned a small bookstore in Carmel, California, and read everything she could to keep up with her customers, many of whom were very astute readers of mystery novels. It was through her reading and interactions with customers that she decided to try writing mysteries.

Judith used her own experiences as a former police officer to create Starletta Duvall, the African American, female homicide lieutenant who is the protagonist of her novels. She is also able to humanize the police officers in her books and address some of the emotional aspects of police work.

Getting That First Book Published

Judith sent her first book to every publisher in New York—and was rejected by all. Without agent representation, publishers were not interested in reading her manuscript. So she got a copy of *Writer's Market* and sent the book to every listed agent who would read unsolicited manuscripts.

Next she decided to try a well-known agent, and even though this agent was not listed as one who accepts unsolicited material, Judith decided to take a chance. She sent the manuscript with a cover letter mentioning one of the agent's famous clients whose work she admires. Although the agent wasn't interested, the associate who read the manuscript eventually started her own agency and, having liked the manuscript, took Judith on as a client.

The entire process of submissions, rejections, and finally being taken on by an agent took just over a year, when *Do Not Go Gently* was accepted by HarperCollins for publication. Judith signed a multibook contract, so the Starletta Duvall series was set. The second book, *The Hoodoo Man*, was purchased from HarperCollins by Random House/Ballantine Books and became part of a new multibook deal with that company.

The Realities of the Work

Judith has difficulty finding anything negative to say about her work, since she genuinely enjoys writing. She does acknowledge, though, that it can be a tough job mainly because the writer is solely responsible for creating the work. She says, "Everything comes from you: characters, dialogue, plot. All of it is conceived, nurtured, and born from you. It's almost like giving birth. In addition, if you're doing a series, there's the added task of 'maturing' your characters and moving them and their lives along. It's very challenging, but I have a real sense of accomplishment at the end of my day."

Judith writes at night, beginning about 8:00 P.M. and working until 3:00 or 4:00 in the morning. She prefers working at night, which is when she feels most energized. She gets up at 11:00 A.M. and runs errands and does chores until her "workday" begins. She doesn't keep strict working hours but writes until she's "empty," generally turning out about twenty pages a night.

Her writing is done in a home office that she considers a fun place to work. Because she likes toys, Judith keeps them on her desk and computer, along with cartoons and photos of family and loved ones. The room is decorated with drawings and knickknacks, as well as framed covers of Judith's books, which provide inspiration for her work. She listens to music while she works, too. Since Starletta Duvall is a Motown fan, she listens to that music when she's working on her detective, but she has a vast collection that reveals a wide range of interests.

Judith says that she doesn't begin writing with an outline, but with an idea, and eventually the characters take over the story. "I realize that sounds a little crazy, but these people are real to me, and because they're real to me, I listen to them," she says. "That's also the key for my readers. Practically every letter I get says 'I know Star' or 'I feel I know these people.' That's a great compliment. If they aren't real to me, they won't be real to the readers, so I give them lives and voices, and I listen.

"In the second novel, *The Hoodoo Man*, my detective asks her partner if he's ever killed anyone in the line of duty. I was all set to say no, but Detective Sargeant Paresi said yes. And I was stunned. I just sat back and transcribed his experience at having had to kill someone during his first year on the street as a patrol officer. When I finished and read it back, I was amazed at the emotion. He said what it felt like to take someone's life, how painful it was for him. Even in a situation where it was kill or be killed. It was almost like being channeled. It's the most fulfilling work I can imagine."

The Upsides and Downsides

Perhaps the greatest upside of Judith's work, she says, is that she is doing something that is enjoyed by others and that touches so many people. She appreciates readers who take the time to write or to meet her and let her know how much they enjoy the books. But she loves writing so much that she says she'd do it even if she were the only one reading it.

What Judith likes least about her work is rewriting. Editors often pick apart a manuscript, cutting parts the author likes and asking for new material, which can be difficult for a writer.

Deadlines can also cause tension, especially when a story involves research. Judith generally enjoys her research, which involves police techniques and developments in forensics, but it can be time-consuming. On the bright side, though, she has the advantage of her former police career and can ask colleagues and other police officers for help.

Advice from a Professional

Judith stresses the need to work hard and to gain an understanding of the financial side of publishing. Your novel might be published, but you might not see any royalty money for several months, or even a year. And remember that large advances have to be repaid before you start earning from the work. She recommends carefully budgeting your money and building a fan base to establish you reputation, and keeping in mind that writing is not a quick path to money and fame.

The best advice Judith can give about actual writing is to write what you know. Start writing down your thoughts and see where they take you. Journaling is a good way for some people to get into the habit of writing every day. Her personal belief is that writing is a gift that can't be taught. A writer can learn the basics of language and study grammar, sentence structure, and spelling, but storytelling is an art that has to come from inside.

Like most professionals, Judith believes that a writer should also be a reader. She says, "If you want to write romances, read them. If you want to write history, whatever, read the genre. Don't steal! But look at how things are phrased, how the dialogue works, check out the characters, see how they make you feel.

"Classic writers are also good teachers. I love to read Mark Twain. His characters and dialogue, though over a hundred years old, are still pertinent and timely. I feel the same way about Dickens. His characters are exciting and mesmerizing, even in today's world. There are also current writers who are masters at plotting, character, and dialogue.

"Bottom line: respect the work—the art—and love it, or do something else."

CLAY REYNOLDS
Novelist
Clay Reynolds is the author of half a dozen novels in genres such as psychological suspense, crime, and historical. His titles include *The Vigil* (Texas Tech University Press, 2000); *Agatite* (St. Martin's Press, 1986; reissued with the title *RAGE*, Signet, 1993); Pulitzer entrant *Franklin's Crossing* (Signet, 1994); *Players* (Pinnacle, 1998); *Monuments* (Texas Tech University Press, 2000); and *The Whore of Hoolian* (Berkley, 2000). He has been writing fiction professionally since 1984.

Getting Started
Clay's writing career began for an interesting reason. He had worked in scholarship, research, and literary criticism for several years, but he found

himself the sole caregiver of his two young children when his wife worked at night outside the home. Since he couldn't get out to the library for research and needed to be alert for most of the evening, he began writing fiction as a way of occupying the hours after his children were asleep.

He completed two novels, *The Vigil* and *Agatite*. He sent *The Vigil* to an agent and *Agatite* to an editor at St. Martin's Press; the following day the editor called to say he had read and wanted to publish *Agatite*. Clay was naturally elated, but he began to worry that the rapid response was a practical joke. He called St. Martin's Press and asked for the editor, who assured him they had indeed just spoken and suggested that Clay get an agent.

Clay phoned the agent to whom he'd sent *The Vigil* and told him about St. Martin's. Although the agent hadn't yet read *The Vigil*, he took Clay on as a client and sold the novel to St. Martin's the next week.

Despite this incredible early success, Clay soon learned that publishing is first and foremost a business. He says, "The quality of a book is the least important consideration in book acquisition and marketing. Its market appeal, demographic target, and price point are far more valuable. Publishers are operating an industry that depends on profit, and a book is a product they can sell."

Subsequent Books

Things didn't go as smoothly with Clay's third novel, *Franklin's Crossing*. When his editor at St. Martin's Press was replaced, the new editor tentatively agreed to buy the new novel, then left the company. The next editor reneged on the verbal agreement, saying he would tell Clay what kind of novels he should be writing. Because this new editor was in charge of the final editing of *Agatite*, Clay waited anxiously until that novel was published.

He and the editor continued to disagree about the way the books were handled; in fact, Clay says that the editor didn't read his books at all. Fortunately, his first St. Martin's editor, who had become president and publisher of Dutton, agreed to buy the new novel. It took Clay three years to complete the research and writing for *Franklin's Crossing*, and two weeks after he submitted the final manuscript, his editor was fired and Dutton was absorbed by Viking Penguin. Two years and three editors later, the novel went to galley pages, where the final editor demanded more changes and cuts.

The most positive aspect of this experience is that Dutton did support the novel, even entering it in the Pulitzer Prize competition. *Franklin's Crossing* won the Violet Crown Award and was runner-up for the Spur Award for Best Western Novel. In addition, Dutton issued a contract for a subsequent historical novel and two crime novels.

Clay wrote and submitted one crime novel, but by that time the industry had changed and Dutton no longer wanted crime or historical novels, and his contracts were canceled. He wrote *Players,* a high-tech psychological thriller with strong crime novel elements, which was published by Carroll and Graf in 1997. Despite outstanding sales, the publisher also decided against another crime novel.

The novel *Monuments* was published by Texas Tech University Press in 2000, and Berkeley published *The Whore of Hoolian* in 2002.

Between writing novels, Clay has also written and edited several nonfiction books and has published short fiction, poetry, original essays, and scholarly material.

The Realities of the Work

For most of his writing career, Clay divided his time between writing and teaching at the University of Texas at Dallas. The university administration was accommodating in allowing him to arrange his schedule so that he would have blocks of time for writing.

He says that although he doesn't feel that he's at his best in the morning, that is usually when he has had the time to write because of his children's schedules. As the kids get older and more independent, however, he is able to switch to writing in the evening, which he prefers. He works exclusively with a computer, which helps to facilitate his other writing and editing work.

Although he's never bored, Clay finds that the work does become tedious at times, especially when he's facing deadlines and feeling the general insecurities that can result from balancing inspiration and talent against craft and ability. He recognizes that writing is a solo occupation and that it is hard work that doesn't respond well to interruptions, distractions, or limitations. He says, "There is no worse enemy of mine than telephone solicitors and telemarketers."

Clay works in a home office, away from television and other distractions. He generally works eight to twelve hours a day. He takes occasional walks, and may nap if he can't come up with an idea. He also reads a great deal.

If he feels that he's on a roll with something, Clay might work eighteen to twenty-four hours straight. He says, "Writer's block is a constant and real companion. It can strike at any time, even in the middle of a sentence. Emotions in writing are very close to the surface and are often very real. They have to be generated and nurtured, but they can never override the intellect. This is hard work, and it requires a daily commitment.

"Writing is not a hobby. It can be fun—it can be marvelous fun—but it's always work, even when it's the most fun."

The Upsides and Downsides

When asked what he likes most about his work, Clay says, "I like writing most when it works. There's no feeling in the world as wonderful as when things are in a groove and the words and ideas fit together in a way you know is original and you hope is profound.

"What I like next best is when I read a review or a letter from someone who has read what I've written, and the reader actually understood what I was trying to do. They don't have to like it. But if they understand it, that's the best part of the whole shooting match."

Clay acknowledges that the high of seeing your words in print or your books in a store fades fairly quickly, since it reminds the author that he'd better get another book published as soon as possible.

What he finds most difficult is the knowledge that no matter how well you write or how much people like your books, failure is still a possibility. The publishing industry changes rapidly, and readers want newer material, which can be very difficult for a writer.

The worst thing about writing for Clay is the feeling that no one understands what you do, except for other writers. "People who read think that writing is just reading turned around backward. They have no idea the special kind of pain that's involved or the amount of work it takes even to complete a short piece of fiction. Everyone thinks that he or she is a writer. All they need is the time to do it, they'll happily assure you. Hearing that repeated over and over is the worst thing there is."

The next worst thing is a financial matter. Clay takes issue with readers who consider books too expensive and don't want to pay full price. He explains that a writer doesn't make any money when his book is purchased from a used store, remainder house, or any other clearinghouse setting. In Clay's opinion, "When you tell a writer you bought the book there, you have just told him that you've taken money out of his pocket."

Earnings

Clay says that an occasional large influx of cash occurs from time to time, and a large contract can bring tens of thousands of dollars at once. But while this may sound like a lot, the money is divided at least in half and spread over a period of six months to two years, and he must deduct from it his federal and state taxes, agency fees, accountant's fees, and insurance payments. There is also the cost of overhead, which includes any office furnishings or a new computer and software upgrades.

"When broken down to an hourly rate, this means that the writer makes mere cents per hour, often less," Clay says. "Rumors of huge contracts worth six figures or more are to some degree accurate. But such contracts represent less than a tenth of one percent of those issued. On average, a writer can expect to make between $10,000 and $20,000 from a first novel, if it's published by a major house in New York, well-publicized, and reviewed in one of the major trades. These earnings will be spread over a period of one to four years in disbursement."

Advice from a Professional

Like most experienced writers, Clay advises against writing for the money. "There's little of it," he says. "The best quality a writer can possess is an independent income or a job that allows you time to write."

He also cautions that a writer must be prepared to spend huge amounts of time alone and to rely on his or her own judgment, opinion, and ability. Writers must also be able to handle rejection and criticism—from editors, agents, the public, and even family and friends. And remember that writers are not celebrities, even when they're famous. In Clay's opinion, "They're ordinarily introverted and somewhat frumpy, ill-mannered and sour-tempered, shabby people, who probably would be happier home alone watching an old movie on the tube than talking to just about anybody."

Clay recommends a strong command of the language and a solid foundation in the rules of grammar. And, like the other writers and agents you've met in this book, he suggests that you read! "You cannot read enough if you do nothing else for every waking minute of the rest of your life," he says. "Read, read, read. Read history, sociology, chemistry, poetry, plays, novels, short stories, quantum physics, geography, psychology, sports accounts, daily newspapers, weekly magazines, monthly journals, and high school yearbooks. Read. Especially read literature. Bestsellers only teach you what's hot, not what's good. You cannot write originally if you don't know what's been written. Then sit down and tell a story. Fiction is a lie with which we tell the truth. Tell your lie. Tell it well. But tell it as a story."

LINDA ADDISON
Poet

By day, Linda Addison is a computer programmer, by night a poet. Her poetry and short stories have appeared in *Asimov's Science Fiction* magazine, *Dark Regions*, *Tomorrow*, *Epitaph*, *White Knuckles*, *Edgar*, *Lore*, *Pirate Writings*, *Tales of the Unanticipated*, *Haiku Headlines*, *Frogpond*, and *Brussels Sprout*.

Linda is also the poetry editor for *Space & Time* magazine, a science fiction (SF)/fantasy/horror publication. She has been writing for more than thirty years and has been with the writer's group Circles in the Hair (CITH) in New York for more than fifteen years. Linda's poetry collection, *Consumed, Reduced to Beautiful Grey Ashes*, published by *Space & Time* in 2001, received a Bram Stoker Award in 2002 in the Poetry Collection category.

The Attraction to Writing

Linda began writing journals in high school and suddenly found herself writing poetry as a means of self-expression. She credits an early habit of reading aloud to herself from the works of such authors as Shakespeare, Poe, Langston Hughes, and others, with helping her to recognize that her thoughts were poetry.

Getting Published

The first time Linda saw her name in print was in her high school newspaper, and she enjoyed the feeling tremendously. Her first professional publication was the appearance of two poems in a magazine called *Just Write*. This was a new magazine, and she was fortunate to be published in the first issue with an entire page to herself.

Since that time, Linda has published dozens of poems. Her proudest accomplishment is the poems she has published in *Asimov's Science Fiction* magazine, which began accepting her work after ten years of rejections. Linda considers this a major achievement because Isaac Asimov was an influence on her writing for many years.

Linda says that to ensure her continued publication, she regularly writes and markets her work. She writes in a journal every day, and she carries a notebook so that she can jot down any interesting images or ideas as they occur. She has learned that memory alone isn't sufficient to recall a particular phrase, but writing a note to herself usually triggers the image later on.

As for marketing, Linda spends time each week checking print and online magazines that list markets. She keeps her own summaries of the markets on index cards, and each week tries to "farm" a new poem from her notes and journals and then list at least three markets for it. "Farming" a poem means rewriting it—Linda writes most of her first drafts on paper, but she rewrites on the computer because she finds it easier to change the physical shape of the poem that way. She can also use the computer's thesaurus to look for fresh words. She tries to do something unusual with her poems as she works on them, which keeps her interested in the work and makes it easier to market.

Linda says that the biggest factor in getting published is simply to keep her poems in the mail. She says, "With a little time spent licking stamps and a lot of thick skin, I've been able to keep the acceptance letters coming."

Writing

Most of Linda's poetry is based in science fiction and horror. She finds that the two genres require different creative skills, and she enjoys both in different ways. She uses her background in mathematics and science for the sci-fi work, and personal reactions to negative events for the horror poems.

Since she works as a computer programmer during the day, Linda does most of her writing in the evening or while commuting back and forth to work. She also likes to spend some time before going to bed writing about something from the day, which might be sparked by something interesting that someone said or something that she read. On weekends, Linda "farms" the writing she's done during the week by looking through her journal and notebook for something of interest. She tries to add a new poem a week to her list of circulating work.

When she's writing science fiction, Linda strives to be as scientifically accurate as possible. Most of her sci-fi works juxtapose hard science against human emotion, often using the question "what if?" to arrive at a different view of things. As an example, she cites her poem "Land Shark," which concerns the possibility of genetic engineering gone awry. The poem was published in *Asimov's Science Fiction*. Like "Land Shark," many of her works have been inspired by things she's seen on nature and science programs.

Linda says that the horror poems come from the dark, emotional side of her creative mind. She explains that she began writing these poems only a few years ago, once she began to feel safe enough to face such darkness. Inspiration might come from her own feelings of anger or from fear based on a memory or a news item. She attempts to use images to invoke the emotion she feels, and she finds that writing these feelings and reactions is a cleansing experience.

Sometimes Linda learns of a special market, such as a magazine looking for poems involving ghosts and machines, and she'll write specifically on that subject. If the magazine doesn't buy the poems, she'll find other markets for them.

Marketing

Linda generally works on marketing on weekends, but she might take one evening during the week to read the market listings and update her cross-listings. She keeps an index card for each poem, which includes the title and number of lines, as well as any possible magazine markets. She records the market and the date she sends a poem out and also notes the magazine's decision and whether the editor offered any helpful comments. She finds that this system helps to keep her work circulating in the mail. She also keeps a folder of printouts of her circulating works so that she has ready access to her poems at all times.

Linda says that the best way to know if your poem will fit a market is to read a sample of the magazine. Rather than purchasing many different magazines, you can look them over at bookstores that encourage browsing.

She has also begun to sell poems to electronic markets and print magazines that accept e-mail submissions. Linda likes the idea that this saves her money on postage, and she also finds that she gets responses faster from these markets.

On the technical side, Linda reminds poets to pay attention to how the work is formatted for submission. Ignoring publishers' guidelines can make you look inexperienced, so it's important to make a good first impression with your submission. If Linda is sending four or more poems, she mails them flat in a large envelope with a smaller SASE enclosed. She marks the poems "disposable" so that she only needs one stamp on the SASE. Print one poem per page, with your name and address in the upper right-hand corner and the line count in the upper left-hand corner.

The Upsides and Downsides

There are two things that Linda particularly loves about writing poetry. She finds great satisfaction, often a healing sensation, in letting words flow from her. "Once the poem is finished," she says, "there's a magical moment when the poem is no longer connected to me and I see it as a first-time reader. The images give me a chill, and I wonder where it came from; that's very enjoyable."

The second thing that Linda loves is seeing her poems in print and knowing that strangers are reading them and hopefully understanding her images and having a reaction to them. She also enjoys doing poetry readings, which provide a welcome change from the solitary writing process. Readings give her an opportunity to share with an audience and see their immediate reactions to the work.

She says that the only aspect of the work that she doesn't enjoy is marketing, which she describes as "necessary work, like washing dishes. If you want to eat, you've got to wash the dishes from the last meal." She knows that the only way she'll see her work in print is to market, write the letters, and mail out her poems, but she admits that she would gladly pay someone to do the marketing if she could afford to.

Earnings

The highest-paying market Linda has sold to is *Asimov's Science Fiction* magazine, which pays $1 a line (poems should not exceed forty lines). She is more commonly paid $5 to $10 a poem. Most magazines pay a flat rate per poem, while some only offer a copy of the magazine.

Linda sends her poetry to the highest-paying markets first, unless she has a special feeling for the magazine—for example, she might feel that some of her poems are perfect for a new publication. It's important to remember that she doesn't support herself writing poetry; her main income comes from computer programming.

Advice from a Professional

Linda feels that because earning money writing poetry is quite difficult, you should be driven by the need to write before attempting to start a career as a poet. She shares some helpful points she learned after she began to write poetry. Keep a daily journal and carry a notebook to capture the images, ideas, and music that you experience each day. Read poetry, aloud when possible. This is particularly helpful when you are rewriting your own poems, since it will help you to hear whether you've captured the music of the poem. Keep a thesaurus nearby to help with your rewriting.

Linda recommends being smart about your marketing strategies. Be sure to send poems to the appropriate markets, and try submitting to new publications, which are often eager to attract poets. As her final word of advice, Linda says, "Don't let any poems stay in the house. Keep them in the mail. A publisher can't buy your poetry if it's on your desk."

THREE HELPFUL TIPS

You realize by now that getting a novel published can be a very long, often difficult process. But don't be discouraged, because if you really believe in your work and aren't afraid to face the competitive market, your novel may very well find a publisher. Here are three tips to keep in mind as you prepare for and write that first novel.

• Be sure to write in a genre you are comfortable with, and be aware of all its requirements. Follow your own interests, and write what you like to read.

• Don't submit your work too quickly. Make sure your manuscript is polished; in fact, when you think it's ready for submission, walk away from it for a while and then read it again. You'll be surprised at how many times you can fine-tune your work. You might also get a professional critique (see Appendix A for resources).

• Become completely familiar with the proper ways of approaching agents and editors. Make sure that your manuscript is professionally prepared and that your query letter succinctly delivers the pertinent information.

C H A P T E R

3

WRITING NONFICTION BOOKS

"There are no dull subjects. There are only dull writers."

—H. L. Mencken

Nonfiction writers have it somewhat easier than aspiring novelists. Of the approximately 100,000 books published each year, 85 percent to 90 percent are in the nonfiction category. This means that nonfiction writers have many more markets to approach, and their chances of breaking in with that first book are much higher. To go one step further, a career as a nonfiction book writer is more than possible, and not just for a few lucky lottery-winner types.

NONFICTION CATEGORIES

Here is a list, culled mostly from the current *Writer's Market* (Writer's Digest Books), of all the possible nonfiction categories you could write in.

Agriculture   Anthropology/Archaeology
Alternative Lifestyles   Art
Americana   Architecture
Animals   Astrology

Autobiography	Law
Automotive	Literary Criticism
Bibliography	Marine Subjects
Biography	Memoirs
Business/Economics	Military/War
Child Guidance/Parenting	Money/Finance
Children's Nonfiction	Multicultural
Coffee-table Books	Multimedia
Communications	Music/Dance
Community/Public Affairs	Nature/Environment
Computers/Electronics	New Age
Consumer Affairs	Philosophy
Contemporary Culture	Photography
Cookbooks	Picture Books
Counseling/Career Guidance	Psychology
Crafts	Real Estate
Creative Nonfiction	Recreation
Educational/Textbooks	Reference
Entertainment/Games	Regional
Ethnic	Religion
Fashion/Beauty	Scholarly
Feminism	Science/Technology
Film/Cinema/Stage	Self-Help
Gardening/Horticulture	Sex
Gay/Lesbian	Social Sciences
Gift Books	Sociology
Government/Politics	Software
Health/Medicine	Spiritual
History	Sports
Hobbies	Technical
House/Home	Translation
How-To	Transportation
Humanities	Travel
Illustrated Books	True Crime
Juvenile Books	Women's Issues/Studies
Labor	World Affairs
Language/Literature	Young Adult

Some categories are fairly broad and can overlap the above-mentioned topics. For example, "how-to" could cover anything from how to build a deck to how to use a particular computer program. "Self-help" could cover parenting, relationships, overcoming addiction, and so on. When looking for possible publishers, remember to look under several different categories your project might fit in.

How you go about marketing your submissions is somewhat easier with nonfiction than with fiction. While new novelists must have a completed project before approaching an editor or agent, nonfiction writers can have an idea with which they can test the waters, before writing the book. Let's see how that's done.

SELLING, THEN WRITING YOUR NONFICTION BOOK

Often nonfiction writers can sell a book based on a detailed proposal even before they actually write the book. If your proposal is well crafted, has all the pertinent information, and convinces the editor you can deliver a professional manuscript on time, you might just find a contract coming your way.

Some editors, however, are reluctant to offer a contract to a writer with no track record or no real expertise in the subject matter. In this case, you have to decide if it's worth the risk to write the book on "spec" (speculation). If you've done your research, know that there's a place for your project on bookstore shelves, and are a competent writer, it might be worth forging ahead.

What isn't a good idea is to write a nonfiction book first, then start looking for possible publishers for it. Just as with fiction, you have to write to the market—know that there's a niche out there within which your book can fit.

The following six steps to getting your nonfiction book published will show you the ideal procedure to follow.

SIX STEPS TO GETTING PUBLISHED

As with writing fiction, there are steps that you should follow to succeed in getting your nonfiction work published.

Step 1: Come Up with an Idea

While this might sound perfectly obvious, it can be a stumbling block. Having a general idea of what you want to write is not enough. You must make sure your topic is viable and tightly focused.

Step 2: Do Your Research

How many other books are out there covering your subject matter? A simple search on the Internet, at the library, or with Books in Print can answer that question right away. If there are dozens and dozens of books on the subject, it could mean your idea isn't new and original, and the topic's been covered ad nauseam.

Don't despair, though. If your book has an original slant, a fresh focus, or a perspective that hasn't been covered, you might be able to keep the project alive. For example, there might be hundreds of books that cover traveling through Europe. But if your book is narrowed down and is, for example, a guide to bike tours on the continent, then perhaps there is room for your title, too. The narrower your focus on a well-published topic, the greater your chances of success.

But don't make your focus too narrow. The fact that there are very few or even no books on your topic in print doesn't necessarily mean guaranteed success. It could also mean there is no interest in the topic, and publishers won't want to take a chance. Say, for example, your bike tour book focuses on only one small city in an area that's difficult for tourists to reach. The audience for this book would be too narrow—and that's why you didn't find other books on the subject.

Checking for competing titles is only half of the research you have to do. You also need to have a good idea of who would buy your book and how this market would be reached. Are you considering a book on pet care? Then you need a rough number of how many pet owners there are in the United States and Canada and how many pet shows are held each year where your book might be sold.

Step 3: Target the Markets

After you've done your initial research and determined that there might be an audience for your book, find publishers you could approach with the project. *The Literary Marketplace*, Writer's Digest's *Writer's Market*, and

The International Directory of Little Magazines and Small Presses are the best places to start. Information about finding these resources is given in Appendix B.

Contact likely candidates and ask them to send you their catalog. Then you can see exactly what they've already published and where your book may or may not fit. Also ask for their writers' guidelines so that if you do decide to approach them, you can offer them exactly what they want. The guidelines will tell you such details as their word count requirements and if they expect authors to provide illustrations.

Step 4: Craft the Query Letter

Just as with writing fiction, your query letter for a nonfiction book must be professionally crafted. The content is different, however. For nonfiction you must include a summary of the book's focus, a rationale for the book (why it should be published), and why you're the one qualified to write the book—all in one page. The query should end with your offer to send a detailed proposal. (See Figure 3.1 for a sample query letter.)

Step 5: Send Out Your Query Letter

Once you have your list of potential publishers, mail your query letter with an SASE to just a few at a time. If you get feedback on your idea, you might discover a need to revise the query. You want to make sure you haven't flooded all the markets and have no publishers left to approach.

Step 6: Craft Your Book Proposal

While you're waiting for those SASEs to come back to your mailbox, get your proposal ready. An excellent guide to help with this is Michael Larsen's *How to Write a Book Proposal* from Writer's Digest Books. In brief, your proposal should include the sections described here.

Your proposal *table of contents* will show what sections you have included in your proposal and on what page of the proposal each can be found. (This is not the table of contents for your proposed book. See "Sample Table of Contents" later in this section for that.) The following topics should be included in the proposal table of contents.

Introduction/Overview. This is your chance to hook the publisher's interest by describing your book and making it sound compelling enough that the publisher will want to read the rest of your proposal.

Competition. You want to highlight a gap in the marketplace that your book can fill. Don't list all the competing titles out there, but show that there is some competition, and that those books don't cover what you plan to focus on.

The Market. In general, it's the publisher's job to know the market—publishers are already well aware of school and public libraries, for example. But, if you know about special outlets for selling your proposed book, mention them here.

Format. In this section explain how your book will be laid out, how many parts there are, how many chapters, whether or not illustrations are required. If you're proposing a cookbook, for example, give the publisher an idea of how many recipes will be in each chapter and what kind and how much additional information will be included with each recipe.

Author Bio. Focus your bio on the areas that show you are qualified to write the book. If your proposed book is a history of a particular region, and you happen to hold a Ph.D. in history and are an expert in the field, then highlight that. If you're proposing a self-help manual for those living "alternative lifestyles," make sure you're a qualified professional who has counseled hundreds, if not thousands, of people on these issues.

What if you're not an expert in any particular field, and you have just your own experiences to draw from? Then you've got a tough sell on your hands. Give your proposal extra credibility by pointing out (both here and in the format section) that you'll be providing quotes and interviews with experts, and consider finding an expert in the field who will coauthor the book with you or provide a foreword.

Sample Table of Contents. Provide a sample table of contents that names each chapter. You can mention a few of the chapter topics, but you don't need to go into great detail here—you'll do that in the next step. The sample table of contents should provide the person considering your proposal with a quick look at what your book will cover.

Chapter Summary. Give a brief, tightly written paragraph or two summarizing the focus of each chapter. Avoid the common mistake of beginning each chapter summary with "Chapter 1 includes, Chapter 2 includes." Jump right into the meat of each chapter.

Sample Chapters. Some proposals include one or two sample chapters, to give the publisher an idea of your book's focus and the style of writing. However, if you're hoping to land a contract based on the proposal, this is a lot of work to do on spec. If you've already written the book, then by all means, include samples. If not, omit this section and wait to be asked.

Cover Letter. If you've sent off a one-page query letter and received responses requesting the detailed proposal you offered, make sure to include a cover letter that performs the following three functions:

- Reminds the publisher that your material is solicited
- Reminds the publisher in a sentence or two what your proposed book is about
- Reminds the publisher who you are and what qualifies you to be proposing this book

Keep the cover letter to less than one page. Make sure you have all your contact information, including your e-mail address and cell phone number. And don't forget to include an SASE if one is requested, for either the return of your proposal or a response.

Writing the Book. If all has gone well—you did your research, sent out your queries, and followed through with requests for your proposal—you might just find yourself with a contract and a due date. Now it's time to write that book. Don't be afraid of discussing the focus or approach with your editor. But, as with any writing project, it involves applying bottom to seat cushion—sitting there and doing it.

SAMPLE QUERY LETTER

The query letter in Figure 3.1 is one this author and her coauthor used to approach the editors at Writer's Digest Books. Although it took two years

Figure 3.1: Sample Query Letter

(On your letterhead with your phone number and e-mail address)
Date

Editor's Name, Title
Publishing House
Address

Dear Editor's Name:

One of the nicest moments a beginning novelist gets to experience is typing the words "The End" on the last page of a manuscript. But for many, the sense of accomplishment can often be short-lived. The manuscript is done, but now what? Market-savvy writers know that a polished manuscript is not the only step in making a good impression with prospective editors or agents; how to approach these publishing professionals can carry as much weight as stellar writing. After studying the available literature, a new writer quickly discovers that, along with sample chapters, cover letters, and SASEs, one of the submission requirements is the synopsis. But what's that?

The now frustrated writer will return from the library or bookstore empty-handed. There are no published guidelines on how to write the novel synopsis. Our proposed book, *Synopses*, will fill that huge gap in the marketplace. We cover the different uses of a synopsis, format, the essential elements, mistakes to avoid, and submission strategies.

But, by far, the most exciting component in our book will be the dozens of actual synopses supplied by well-known writers. We have already received contributions from Elmore Leonard, Dick Francis, and Marilyn Campbell and are expecting more. In addition, we have interviewed selected editors and agents for comments on what they look for in a synopsis. These interviews and sample synopses, along with comments from the contributing authors on when, why, and how they wrote them, will guide readers through an often difficult and confusing process and will also enhance the promotability of our book.

Both of us come into contact with several hundred beginning writers each year, through writers' workshops and seminars, through the Fiction Writer's Connection membership, through our newsletters, and through referrals. Some of the most frequent questions we receive concern the "dreaded synopsis." Why do we need it? What is it for? What does it look like? How do we write it?

We have designed Synopses to answer those questions, and more.

May we send you a full proposal?

Sincerely,

Blythe Camenson and Marshall J. Cook

---

and a broadening of the book's focus (it now covers every aspect of getting your novel published, not just the synopsis), Writer's Digest published the book with the revised title, *Your Novel Proposal: From Creation to Contract.*

DO YOU NEED AN AGENT?

You've just read the six steps to getting published and now you're wondering why contacting agents was not mentioned. While fiction writers usually fare better with an agent representing them, nonfiction writers can often approach publishers alone. There are many more publishers who handle nonfiction than fiction, and they are often open to accepting submissions directly from authors. In fact, many of the smaller presses rarely are approached by agents and are not used to working with them. This is in part because most agents prefer to work with the "big guys," where advances and subsequent print runs and sales are usually higher.

If your project is of global interest, you could approach agents first—following the same six steps mentioned earlier. But if your project fits more into a niche market, don't be hesitant to go it alone.

For more information on agents, see Chapter 2.

POTENTIAL EARNINGS

As with novels, some contracts for nonfiction books provide an advance against royalties. Others offer a "work-for-hire" or flat fee arrangement, which means that whatever you're paid up front for the book is all the money you'll see. If the book goes on to be a bestseller, your bank balance will have no cause to celebrate.

Sometimes you have no choice, and, if you think sales might be minimal, such as with a small press that has limited distribution, a flat fee is not a bad idea.

If the publisher is confident, planning a fairly large initial press run of 10,000 or more, and offers an advance against royalties, you can hope to see some checks down the road once the advance is earned back. (Statements are usually issued two times a year, and it could be a year or so before sales have earned back the advance.)

Dollar amounts are hard to pinpoint. Some of the small presses offer no advance at all, just a royalty percentage. With this scenario, you have no money coming in while you're writing the book, but at least you won't have to wait to earn back a nonexistent advance. In theory, you should receive your first check with the next royalty period, probably six months from the time your book is on the market.

Other small presses offer advances that range from $500 to $3,000 or so. A large publisher might advance a new writer as high as $10,000 to $25,000, and sometimes more if it's a hot topic and the sales team predicts healthy sales. According to the 2006 *Writer's Market* survey, the average earnings for nonfiction book writing (advance against royalties) was $14,475, with a low of $2,000 and a high figure of $75,000.

AVOIDING FADS

You're back at the Six Steps to Getting Published section, looking at Step 1. You've got an idea and it's hot. You want to stress in your query letter just how hot the topic is—and that the publisher should act fast. That's what you want to do, but you won't.

Publishers traditionally take up to a year or more for a book to see print. What's hot now will be old news by then, so be sure to think about publication dates before pitching your idea. While you might be fascinated by a current issue, make sure that your research includes some forward projections—you may find clues that your topic will fizzle within the next year or so. For example, if you're considering writing about the phenomenon of reality television shows, work at finding out what the networks are planning for the next season—you don't want to find that the wave has crested just as your book is being published.

Publishers sometimes do put out quickie books related to such topics as celebrity antics or a major political issue. Paris Hilton and the Iraq War come to mind as examples. But nine times out of ten, publishers contact a writer they already know to produce that kind of book.

SELLING THAT SECOND BOOK

If you've followed the six-step program mentioned earlier in this chapter, you've collected a slew of publisher catalogs. Notice how many publishers produce books in a series. Series books cover all sorts of categories: gardening, travel, careers, cooking, and so on. Examine these carefully to see where the gaps are—gaps that you can fill. A publisher with a sports line, for example, has every book under the sun—except windsurfing. You just happen to know a lot about the subject and would love to produce a book on it.

Studying publisher catalogs works well for coming up with ideas for a first book, but it can also help with future titles, too. Perhaps your first book fit into your publisher's series. You've delivered an outstanding manuscript, you've developed a wonderful rapport with your editor, and now you see ideas for more books to round out their list. At this point, it is perfectly acceptable to make a quick call to your editor to discuss the possibility of additional contracts for you. After listening to your ideas, your editor might tell you those projects are already under contract. Or you might receive a suggestion to send in a miniproposal and sample table of contents.

Once you've established a working relationship with an editor, that second, third, and even fourth book is much easier to pitch and sell.

And if your first book was a one-hit wonder for that particular publisher, move on. You still have a book to your name, which will add credibility to your proposals to other publishers.

FIRSTHAND ACCOUNTS

Two nonfiction writers have shared their experiences for this book. Read on to see how they got started.

MARTHA HOLLIS
Nonfiction Book Writer
Martha Hollis has a dozen food, travel, and computer technology books to her credit, including the following titles: *The International Breakfast Book* (Macmillan, 1997); *Cooking with the Young and the Restless* (Rutledge Hill Press, 1997); *Culinary Secrets of Great Virginia Chefs* (Rutledge Hill Press, 1995); *Palate Pleasures: The Best Restaurants of Hampton Roads* (LeFleur Press, 1994); and *Whole Grain Goodies* (LeFleur Press, 1990).

She has a Ph.D. in decision and information sciences from Arizona State University, and in 2006 she was named director of distance learning at Embry-Riddle Aeronautical University in Daytona Beach, Florida.

Getting Started

Martha was initially fascinated with the idea of computers for home use and left her job as professor of decision sciences at the University of San Francisco to write the book *High Tech Hits Home*. She decided that she also wanted to write about food and travel, so she attended chef school full-time for two years and traveled extensively.

To market her first book, Martha sent about twenty proposals directly to publishers of computer books, without using an agent. After about four months, she received an acceptance from CBS Computer Books.

Martha says that the food book genre is very tough, with a great deal of competition. She self-published five books that she marketed through a whole-food market in Dallas while teaching cooking classes, an experience that she describes as a tough way to earn money.

As a trained chef, Martha was invited to edit a collection of recipes from fifty other chefs of the American Culinary Federation (ACF). She tested all the recipes with ingredients provided or paid for by the chefs. Martha found a publisher for *Culinary Secrets of Great Virginia Chefs* by sending proposal packages, which took more than two years. She handled the contract arrangement herself.

Martha used an agent for the first time for *The International Breakfast Book*, and she found that her advance was significantly higher than for previous books. Her next book, *Cooking with the Young and the Restless*, was requested by Rutledge Hill Press, the publisher that put out the ACF book.

What the Work Is Really Like

On most days, Martha heads directly to her home office when she gets up. She answers e-mail as her writing warm-up, then writes for several hours, taking a break for lunch. Each day includes some exercise by hiking, skiing, golfing, or working in her garden.

As a food and travel writer, Martha needs to visit destinations often, and she tries to schedule a five- or six-day trip at least once a month. For a set project such as *The International Breakfast Book*, she arranges the travel herself. In this case, her research involved about three years of periodic travel and a final three-month trip through Europe and Africa, with a computer and photography equipment in a backpack and minimal clothes in a small suitcase. She arranged to have most of the travel expenses paid for by the hospitality client, such as a hotel or airline.

For projects that she is researching on spec, without an assignment, Martha takes press trips arranged by public relations firms, international travel offices, or other travel promoters such as tour operators, hotels, luxury resorts, chambers of commerce, and food trade associations. She recommends this as a great way to gather information at a very low cost.

Once the traveling is finished, Martha downloads images from her digital camera, catalogs slides after processing and organizing her notes, and finally begins to write. For a press trip, she likes to write an immediate magazine or Internet article, saving her favorite parts of the research for her next proposed book.

When she's working on technical books, Martha tests software and computer applications. To update her high-tech book, she worked with culinary software, music learning and composing software, and home and garden design packages. She feels fortunate to be working with the "fun" side of computing.

The Upsides

Martha loves having the freedom to choose her major projects and to propose books on topics that interest her. She finds the associated research, discovery, and learning to be an ongoing and fun process.

She also enjoys the atmosphere of working at home, especially since she lives on a mountaintop in a rural area. Using an answering machine to take calls allows her to work uninterrupted for long periods, which is particularly important when facing a deadline. She finds being at home fun, since she can take a break by doing household chores or turning the compost pile or working in one of her gardens.

Another plus is the ability to travel at minimal expense and dine in fine restaurants, as well as the adventure-travel experiences, such as white-water rafting and weeklong hikes. Meeting people from all walks of life is also an important benefit.

"Another upside is the 'amazing factor,'" Martha says. "Several years after a book is published, I sometimes read a portion and am amazed that God has given me the gift of writing. Especially in food and travel books, I feel that I am a conduit for people who would not have been otherwise heard.

"During the research phase for the *Breakfast Book*, people wanted to tell me what they had in the morning. They wanted to share their traditions.

They were excited that others were interested. They were delighted to be included. It amazed me the responses I received from the finished product. This particular book has helped spread joy in the world."

The Downsides

Martha finds the most difficult part of her job to be constant rejection by publishers and editors, and she particularly dislikes being told that a particular book proposal has no marketing appeal. She has tried self-publishing but found both the distribution and promotion difficult. Her submissions are now handled by an agent, who circulates about twenty proposals a year with about a 5 percent acceptance rate.

Another downside to writing is the uneven cash flow. Martha has learned to take on other assignments, such as newspaper work or magazine articles, to meet short-term cash needs. In addition, the need to purchase her own health insurance and the responsibility to pay all the bills herself are frustrating.

Martha also says that she misses having lunch with friends on a regular basis, since it's often difficult to stop working and maintain a social life. Fortunately, she has to test many recipes, which she does at dinner parties. She also tries to select press trips that will allow her to be with friends.

Advice from a Professional

Martha recommends taking college writing courses. She also advocates traveling as often as possible and mastering foreign languages.

She feels that a successful nonfiction writer should posses the qualities of curiosity, tenacity, and patience. Being a self-starter will also serve you well, as will being attentive to everything around you and asking a lot of questions. Be totally honest with your subjects and clients, and be sure to maintain your integrity. People skills are mandatory—smile frequently and listen carefully. Be prepared with interviews, do the background research, and check all your sources. Don't be afraid to ask others for help when you need it.

Martha also suggests having excellent grammar and spelling skills, as well as impeccable organizational skills. She believes that a well-rounded background is essential for success, especially in basic business, since you will have to keep your own financial records, conduct your own marketing, and find new outlets for your work.

On the practical side, she recommends knowing how to upgrade and repair your own computer, or finding someone you trust who can do this for you.

"To get started, write every chance you get," Martha says. "Letters and e-mails to friends and relatives are excellent practice vehicles. Volunteer to write short pieces for newsletters in your community such as at your church or a local museum. I used to write for an opera guild in Dallas and received tons of exposure from it. I also edited a cookbook for a master gardener group. Bartering was and still is helpful because you can trade your writing skills for something you need or want."

JAN GOLDBERG
Nonfiction Book Writer
Jan Goldberg is a full-time writer of nonfiction books and articles. Her articles have appeared in more than two hundred publications, including *Complete Woman*, *Chicago Parent*, and *Opportunity Magazine*. To date she has more than a dozen books in print, including four Hi-Low career books for children and several career titles for McGraw-Hill (*Careers in Journalism*, *Great Jobs for Music Majors*, *Careers for Adventurous Types and Other Go-Getters*, *On the Job: Real People Working in Communications*, and more).

Getting Started

Jan says that writing was her first love. As a child, she took weekend trips to visit her grandfather, a bookbinder, and was enthralled by the excitement of the process. It was this early exposure that made her decide that she would somehow work with books and writing.

After teaching for several years, she realized that it was writing that still interested her. She began with poetry, and then wrote book reviews. She considered doing some educational writing and made contacts at Scott Foresman and Addison Wesley publishers, for whom she wrote textbooks and activity workbooks. The more she wrote, the more she realized that she preferred writing to teaching.

Jan contacted an educational publisher that handled magazines, and she began to write for *Modern Health* and *Career World*. She next began writing career books for NTC/Contemporary Publishing Group (later acquired by McGraw-Hill), and soon branched out to other publications as well.

The Reality of the Work

Jan considers hers to be among the most interesting of jobs, particularly because she writes both books and articles on a wide variety of topics. She never gets bored, and she says that researching new subjects makes her feel like an explorer venturing into new territory each time she approaches a new topic.

A typical day for Jan includes many tasks, such as contacting editors, responding to e-mail, doing research (which might include visiting a library, using the Internet, or making telephone inquiries), and actual writing. All of her work is done with an eye to the future, because she likes to plan what projects she will be working on later as well as keeping up with the various stages of her current work.

The Upsides and Downsides

"The good part of all of this is that I can call my own shots and make my own schedule," Jan says. "The bad part is the same, because to meet your obligations and do a good job, you really have to put in a lot of time. Some days could be twelve-hour days, and on other days, depending on deadlines and how many projects I have going on, I might be able to take some time off. Because I work from a home office, I can work whenever I want. But because the work is always there, I never quite get away from it."

Another downside of the job is the entrepreneurial aspect of the work. Jan is solely responsible for billing, record keeping, maintaining her filing systems, and of course, marketing her work. She finds the most difficult part of her job to be negotiating contracts and trying to collect money that's owed her.

What she likes most is the anticipation of new projects and ideas and having the opportunity to be creative and do new things. But in reality, writing is hard work, and it isn't always fun.

Advice from a Professional

Jan recommends that you have a lot of projects going on simultaneously if you hope to make a living by writing. As a novice, you must be patient, since getting established is a slow process. You need to be patient and have lots of discipline, and you can't expect too much too soon.

"I've never really figured out an hourly wage for myself, but writing in general is not a high-paying profession," she cautions. "If you want to really make tons of money, you'd probably want to choose another career. Before you think about quitting your day job, you need to be sure how much money you'll be able to make to support yourself."

THREE HELPFUL TIPS

Based on what you've just read in this chapter, you know that there are steps you can take to get started in your career as a nonfiction author. Here are three things to keep in mind as you work.

• Do the necessary research before you start writing. Even before you research your topic, research the market to learn where your work might find the best audience.

• Learn the ins and outs of writing professional query letters and book proposals that will attract interest in your work.

• Once your work has been accepted and published, develop a good working relationship with your editor.

CHAPTER 4

FREELANCE WRITING FOR MAGAZINES AND NEWSPAPERS

"As an entrepreneur you have to work only half a day—and you get to decide which twelve hours it is."
—Source Unknown

Not all writers write books. Some prefer to work on shorter pieces that appear in a variety of publications, such as magazines, newspapers, and newsletters. Freelance magazine and newspaper writers are self-employed and often work from a home office just as novelists and nonfiction book writers do. They generally submit work to more than one publication, although after getting established, they are often able to develop relationships with different editors that ensure ongoing assignments.

Freelance writers study the various publications for style and content and then try to meet the needs of those publications by proposing articles on appropriate topics. They spend as much time marketing their work as they do writing it—sometimes more.

(Freelancers who write in other fields such as advertising, public relations, or technical writing are covered in other chapters in this book.)

DIFFERENT KINDS OF ARTICLES

Articles fall into two broad categories: those that educate and those that
entertain. Here is just a small sampling of the topics covered in magazine articles:

Art	Hobbies
Aviation	Humor
Business/Finance	Military
Careers	Nature
Child Care	Pets
Computers	Photography
Contemporary Culture	Politics
Entertainment	Psychology/Self-Help
Food	Retirement
Gardening	Science
General Interest	Sports
Health	Travel

(For a more detailed list of topics, see Chapter 3.)

Newspapers are also markets for freelance writers. The following are
departments that freelancers often write for:

Business	Fashion
Books	Finance
Entertainment	Food
Health	Lifestyles/Features
Science	Travel
Education	

THE ELEMENTS OF AN ARTICLE

Although the subject matter can be very different, most articles include
many of the same elements. They all start with an interesting *hook*, the first
paragraph that grabs the reader's (and the editor's) attention. They use
quotes from real people or experts, cite important facts, give examples, and
sometimes include amusing anecdotes or experiences.

Some articles have *sidebars*, additional information that doesn't fit in the body of the article but is important for readers to know. Examples of sidebars are a salary survey for a career article, "how to get there" information for a travel piece, or a recipe to accompany a cooking article.

The *style* or *tone* of an article will vary according to the publication. Some editors prefer a casual tone that speaks directly to the reader; others prefer a more formal voice.

The *content*, of course, would be specific to the particular publication. Travel magazines and newspaper travel sections, for example, print articles on various locales, tips on how to save money when traveling, how to be prepared for security issues, or some other aspect of travel. Certain travel publications use only first-person personal-experience pieces; others prefer third person. Some cover only U.S. destinations; others are markets for exotic travel articles.

By studying a publication and sending for its writers' guidelines (a simple request with an SASE [self-addressed, stamped envelope] will quickly have information in the mail to you, or the guidelines might be available online), you can see the style, word count, focus, and approach they prefer.

HOW TO GET THAT FIRST ARTICLE PUBLISHED

There are a few steps you can take to help put you on the road to success.

Study the Publications

Before starting, read as many publications as you can, and in particular, those you would like to write for. Send for sample copies, spend time at the library, or browse through the racks of newsstands. Look online for publications that interest you. It's never a good idea to send an article to a publication you're not familiar with—if you miss the tone or send 2,000 words when they want only 1,000, you might kill your chances for future acceptance.

Some freelancers are generalists and write on a variety of topics, covering whatever strikes their fancy. They have a wide range of interests and prefer the variety. Others are specialists and focus their work in one or two particular areas, and establish a reputation as experienced writers in those areas.

While specialists limit the number of publications for which they can write, they often establish relationships with editors more quickly and have an easier time getting assignments.

Decide What to Write

Once you have decided what you want to write about, you can proceed in two ways:

• You can write the entire article on speculation, send it off to appropriate editors, and hope they like your topic. On-spec writing can be time-consuming and may not necessarily pay off, but new writers don't often have a choice and have to write on spec in order to establish themselves. Editors are often unwilling to give an assignment to a writer without a track record. They want to be sure you can deliver a professional, polished manuscript, and on time, before they will hire you.

• The second approach is to first write a query letter, a miniproposal, to see if the editor is interested in your idea. Query letters will save you the time of writing articles you might have difficulty selling. Only once you're given a definite assignment do you then proceed. See "The Elements of a Query Letter" later in this chapter for more on query letters.

DO YOU NEED AN AGENT?

This is where freelancers go it alone. Most agents don't handle articles, except those written by one of their famous clients who also write books. You can see how much work is involved in selling an article. At 15 percent of $150 to $2,000 or so, the commission is not big enough to make it worthwhile for an agent to enter this arena.

MARKETING YOUR WORK

Aggressive marketing is an important factor in a successful freelance career. The more query letters or articles you have circulating, the better your chances of landing assignments. Go through market guides (see

Appendix B) and note the possible markets for your work. Send out query letters on a regular basis—full-time freelancers report that they send out forty to fifty query letters a week. That's a lot of work, but it's the commitment you'll have to make to establish your career. On the bright side, however, not all query letters are for brand-new article ideas.

Resales

Writing an article, selling it to a publication, and then writing another article to sell to the same or another publication is a slow way to earn a living. Successful freelancers count on being able to sell a single article to more than one source, so when you come up with an article idea you should plan ahead and consider how many different markets the article can target.

Unless a publication has bought all rights, and you don't want to sell all the rights to your articles (see later in this chapter for more information on rights), you are free to resell your article as often as you can. However, the rule is that you must approach only noncompeting markets. For example, your travel piece on "Visiting Civil War Battlefields" could appear in the *Boston Globe* and the *San Francisco Chronicle*, two newspapers that do not share the same readership. But your piece on "Tips for a Safe Campsite" could not appear in both *Camping Life* and *Backpacker* magazines, because they do share the same audience.

Reslant and Resell

Although you can't sell the same article to competing publications, doing just a little extra work will make it possible to resell your pieces to similar markets. For example, you've written a piece on "Ten Tips for Keeping Your Cat Healthy" and sent it off to either *Cat Fancy* or *Cats Magazine*. Now it's time to take a second look at the article. It probably wouldn't take much work to reslant and come up with "Ten Tips for Keeping Your Dog Healthy"—or your horse, or your aquarium, or your pet python.

For every pet there's probably a publication. A quick look at the newsstand or through the market guides will let you know what's out there. A few phone calls to experts in the various fields will give you quotes tailor-made to each article. Or better yet, when talking to that small-pet veterinarian, plan ahead and ask not only about cats but also about dogs and other animals of interest.

Religious publications are abundant and make very good markets for reslanted articles. *Spiritual Life*, a magazine targeted mostly to a Catholic readership, might use an article on contemporary spirituality. So might the *SCP Journal*, geared toward nonbelievers. Although the publications may carry similar articles, they're both fair game because they have different readership.

Spoking

Another way to come up with enough article ideas to keep you in business is spoking. Generally, when writers conduct research for an article, they end up collecting more information than they can possibly use in one story. Savvy writers use that extra research to spin off, or "spoke," other article ideas. A successful writer once said, "Give me a city block to write about, and I can support myself for a year; give me a whole city, and I can support myself writing about it for the rest of my life."

The idea of spoking is based on the spokes of a wheel. Suppose you want to research the effects of Hurricane Katrina on New Orleans. Figure 4.1 is a diagram of a wheel showing how you can spoke several articles out of the hub's main topic—how the hurricane has affected various aspects of the culture and neighborhoods of New Orleans.

Figure 4.1: Katrina's Effects on New Orleans

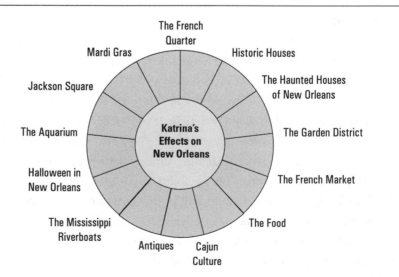

Keeping Track of Your Submissions

Accurate record keeping is an important aspect of your writing business. You don't want to submit the same article twice to the same editor. Develop a system that allows you to keep track of possible markets, submission dates, responses, publication dates, and payment and rights information.

Some writers use index cards (see the profile of poet Linda Addison in Chapter 2), others use computer software specifically designed for this purpose. The more organized you are, the more successful you'll be.

Marketing Your Work Online

The Internet can be one of your most powerful—and inexpensive—tools for attracting attention to your work. In the article "Online PR: Creating a Buzz Without a Budget," from the 2006 *Writer's Market*, full-time freelancer Kelly Milner Halls outlines seven steps to promoting your work without spending a lot of money.

- **Your website.** Experts recommend setting up a website where you can store all the information essential to your work, such as your biographical information, list of works, and press kit. Anyone who is interested in your work or who requests a document can be directed right to the site. Many companies offer inexpensive services for creating and maintaining professional websites.
- **Electronic press kit.** This will save the time and money of mailing kits to individual editors or agents, who can receive the information by e-mail instead. An electronic press kit should include a brief, current author bio, titles of past work, and a list of any awards or interests you would like known. You can also post photos of yourself that will make the kit more noticeable. Last but not least, list all of your contact information.
- **Online newsletter.** Experts advise that an online newsletter is a good way to attract people to your site and to keep them interested in your work. This can be a time-consuming endeavor, though, and it can also take a while to get the word out and find enough subscribers.
- **Free advertising.** Many writers take advantage of Internet chats and interviews to draw attention to their work. Some even offer free article submissions. Although this last idea might seem counterproductive, it can be a very good way of making people aware of your talents and finding some paying assignments.

• **Search engines.** If you register your site with a search engine, it will come up at the top of the list of hits when someone runs a search in your subject. You can do this free at the search engine's home page.

• **E-mail.** Sending targeted e-mail is another way to gain attention for your work. This involves sending e-mail to those in your address book, based on their identified interests. E-mail is much faster and less expensive than sending notices by mail.

• **Print media.** Electronically submit any good reviews or other positive press to the media. Send your press release to newspaper and magazine book sections, as well as to other sections, such as lifestyle, business, family, health, or any other area where it might be appropriate.

THE ELEMENTS OF A QUERY LETTER

A query letter for an article is similar to one for a nonfiction book. The best queries are one page in length (single-spaced) and start with a hook— perhaps the first paragraph of your article—to grab the editor's attention. The hook is the focus of your piece, the slant that makes it different from all the other articles out there. In the body of your query letter you explain your rationale for the piece and your approach—whether you'll be using expert quotes, for example. The bio section of the letter provides your related credits and explains why you are qualified to write this particular piece. You close by asking simply, "May I have the assignment?"

The query letter in Figure 4.2 proposed an article that was ultimately published in several noncompeting newspaper travel sections. It could also be targeted toward architecture or history magazines.

RIGHTS

When you sell an article to a magazine or newspaper you are offering that publication one of the several types of rights.

First North American Rights
This type of rights means the publication that wants to print your material opts for the right to go to press with your work before anyone else does.

(On your letterhead with your phone number and e-mail address)

Date

Editor's Name, Title
Magazine
Address

Dear Editor's Name,

Most people think of Miami Beach as the place where everyone's grandmother lives. For a long time Collins Avenue and Ocean Drive, packed with residential hotels and condominiums, did cater to the over-sixty set. But in the last fifteen years the demographics, as well as the topography, have been changing.

"Miami Beach is an exciting place to live these days," says Jeff Donnelly, volunteer tour guide for the Miami Design Preservation League. "Young professionals, artists, models, movie production people—they're all flocking here now. We've become very chic."

The old establishments, once painted white and trimmed with only powder blue, aquamarine, or the peaches and pinks of aging flamingos, have now received fresh face-lifts and glow with a contemporary pastel palette. Bands of lavender, blue, yellow, aqua, and a whole spectrum of pinks whimsically decorate oceanfront hotels, sidewalk cafés, model agencies, and apartment buildings. Miami Beach can boast of the largest concentration of Art Deco buildings in the country; over 800 contribute to the historic and architectural nature of the Art Deco District. The result is a Disneyesque urban streetscape, as fanciful as Victorian gingerbread, with the promise of campy humor and fun.

I would like to propose a 1,200-word article, called "Beyond the Beach," covering this exciting section of Miami. Color slides are also available.

I am a freelance writer specializing in travel. My articles and photographs have appeared in over 100 publications including *Newsday, Fort Lauderdale Sun-Sentinel,* Gulf Air's inflight, *San Diego Union, San Francisco Examiner, International Living, Accent, AAA Going Places, British Heritage,* and various others.

May I have the assignment?

Sincerely,

Blythe Camenson

Most big magazines such as *Modern Bride* or *Family Circle* will prefer to purchase first rights from you. You must wait—sometimes six months to a year—for your article to appear in print before you can sell it elsewhere. If your article never appears in print, which sometimes happens, you might not be able to sell that piece to another publication, ever, unless you're successful at renegotiating the rights you've sold.

All Rights

All rights means just what you think. The publication is purchasing your article outright, and once you sell it, you no longer own it and cannot sell it elsewhere. Many national magazines such as *Cosmopolitan* prefer to buy all rights, but they usually pay enough to make this worthwhile—$1 to $2 a word.

Sometimes, though, a magazine with a much smaller circulation and a smaller budget for paying freelancers insists on all rights; in this case it isn't worthwhile, since freelancers depend on resales to earn their livings. But don't give up right away if a publication wants all rights. Sometimes rights are negotiable, and a letter or phone call back offering first rights or one-time rights might turn out to be acceptable.

One-Time Rights

Ideally, these are the best rights to sell. Most newspapers and many specialty magazines or newsletters request only one-time rights. Again, this means just what it says. They are buying the right to print your article one time.

Second or Reprint Rights

Some publications don't mind if your article has appeared elsewhere. *Reader's Digest*, for example, often uses reprints, as do some smaller publications that reach only a narrow audience.

Electronic Rights

Electronic rights generally means the right to publish your work on the Internet. This is still an emerging area and can be controversial. Some publishers buying first rights for their print publications have also posted the work online, without additional payment to the writers. Make sure you know what rights you are selling, and when in doubt, ask. If the deal doesn't sound like a good one, you can always say no.

It is a well-established fact that writers, for the most part, are underpaid. It's true that specialists in certain fields who have developed an expertise and a good reputation often make more money than generalists. Business and technology publications, for example, tend to pay more than those in other fields. But still, surveys conducted by the Author's Guild, National Writers Union, and others suggest that only 15 percent of freelancers earn more than $35,000 a year.

Publications usually pay by the word—anywhere from about eight cents up to $4, or an average of about $1.25 per word. This doesn't mean you can earn more money by writing longer articles or padding your piece with extra words. In their guidelines publications state their minimum and maximum word-count requirements, and the editors are certainly professional enough to recognize padding when they see it.

Other publications pay a flat fee—which could be anywhere from $25 to $1,000 or more for an article, with national magazines at the top of the scale. That's why it's much harder to break into these markets—the competition is fierce, and many of them work only with staff writers. (See Chapter 5.)

Some smaller publications pay only with complimentary copies and a byline. Once you query an idea and are given the assignment, discussing payment is usually the next step. Negotiating for more money at this point is not inappropriate. In fact, editors often say they are quite willing to negotiate—and are surprised more writers don't come out and ask for higher fees.

According to the 2006 *Writer's Market* survey, some freelancers who wrote consumer magazine feature articles earned an average of $1,842 per project (the high salary was $7,500, and the low was $150). Others were paid an average of $1.24 per word. For a feature article in a trade journal, the average hourly rate was $122, the average rate per project was $1,412, and the average rate per word was $1.23.

Unfortunately, too many writers go into this business not fully understanding that it is a business. Their expertise is with the written word, not with finances. But to be a successful freelancer, you have to overcome that mind-set, develop a strong business sense, and remember you are selling a valuable product. There is definitely a lot of competition—other writers are selling equally valuable products, and editors can pick and choose whom to work with. But, if you approach the subject with tact and confidence, you won't turn off an editor and send him or her looking elsewhere. The editor has chosen your article and might even have given you input into its contents, and there is no reason you shouldn't be fairly compensated for it.

Having said that, some of the smaller publications just don't have the budget to pay you what your piece may be worth. If a byline and a credit are important to you, go ahead with the sale, but be sure to negotiate one-time rights so you can sell the piece elsewhere for additional income.

Some publications will accept photographs or other illustrations with your article and pay you for each one. Sometimes you'll earn more for your photos than the actual article! One travel writer, who was also an accomplished photographer, realized this early on and stopped writing articles to focus on creating a stock library of color slides to supply to magazines and newspapers.

As mentioned earlier, resales are the bread and butter for freelance writers. When investigating ideas for articles, keep resale and reslant possibilities in mind. You'll make more money, and in a cost-efficient manner, selling one article to ten different publications than you will writing ten different pieces and trying to market each of them just once.

It is important to remember that publishers are notoriously slow to pay for your material. Articles are usually paid for in one of two ways: upon acceptance or upon publication. "Upon acceptance" could mean the check will be cut right away, or it could mean four to six weeks later, based on the schedule of the accounting department. "Upon publication" means that your check will not be issued until the article appears in print, which could be six months to a year from the time you received your acceptance letter. Often your check will be mailed to you with a sample copy of the issue in which your material appears. With this long lag, you can see how important it is to have as many articles as possible circulating to different publications.

Unfortunately, sometimes your check just doesn't seem to be in the mail as promised. If repeated phone calls and reminder notes to editors don't work, try contacting the accounting department directly. It is rare for a publication to out-and-out stiff a writer. Sometimes slow payment or nonpayment can just mean a poorly organized staff.

Or it could mean the publication is about to fold or has already gone out of business. If a publication has gone under—either before or after your article has appeared—there is not much you can do about it. Sure, you can pursue legal action, but chances are you are not in the same state as the publication, and the legal fees would end up costing you more than any money you might collect.

Occasionally a publication might purchase your article and promise to run it, then for a variety of reasons decide not to use it after all. Maybe an on-spec article they like better and on the same topic just arrived, or they changed the focus of the publication, or they decided a topic was too controversial or is now passé. When this happens some publications pay a kill fee—perhaps 15 percent to 25 percent of the agreed-upon fee for the article. This should be paid willingly and amicably if their guidelines state that they do offer a kill fee. But at least one editor has been quoted as saying, "Yes, we pay kill fees, but then we wouldn't work with that writer again." It's not fair, but again, there's not much you can do about it. Over time you will learn to pick and choose the editors you submit to and continue to work with. Establishing good relationships with editors is in part how successful writers keep those assignments and checks coming in.

FIRSTHAND ACCOUNTS

Read what the following professional freelancers have to say about their careers, and see whether you think you can succeed in this challenging line of work.

JOSEPH HAYES
Freelance Features Writer
Joseph Hayes writes features for a variety of magazines and newspapers. His articles cover people, food, computers and technology, travel, music, and writing about writing. His work has appeared in the following publications: *Fiction Writers Guideline, Gila Queen's Guide to Markets, Inklings/Inkspot, iUniverse.com Nonfiction Industry Newsletter, January* magazine, *Jerusalem Report, MaximumPC, Moments Aboard Spirit Airlines,* My Matcher.com, *Orlando Magazine, The Orlando Sentinel, Poets & Writers, savvy-HEALTH, Venture Woman,* and *Writer's Journal.* His first article was published in January 1997.

Getting Started
After working for many years as a corporate sales trainer, Joseph developed a skill for translating complicated technical terms and processes into

understandable language. Although his first love is fiction writing, he has been able to combine his talents to write creative nonfiction.

He began his career by contacting a regional editor at his local newspaper with suggestions about several concrete story ideas within the community. The editor liked one of the ideas and asked him to write it, and he's been writing steadily ever since.

The Reality of the Work

Joseph is primarily concerned with personal accountability, weighing the need for paying assignments against social responsibility. He is pleased to say that so far, he has not taken any assignment just because it pays. On the professional side, his duties are to meet deadlines, to deliver the best work possible regardless of the subject matter, and to maintain contact with editors throughout an assignment.

He loves the work, despite long hours and occasional gaps between paydays. In Joseph's opinion, he is being paid to do what he's always wanted to, and he has many opportunities to meet people he wouldn't ordinarily get to know.

He writes mostly about regular people who do extraordinary things, such as a man who sells UFO abduction insurance, a woman who takes photographs of people's auras, or a former police officer who teaches the bagpipes. His travel articles are about places a tourist wouldn't normally visit, and his technology pieces are based on helping people understand what modern technology means to them. Joseph says, "Bottom line, I'm a storyteller, whether I'm doing it in a piece of fiction or a newspaper."

Most of his work comes from queries that he sends out to editors. If he's pitching an idea to an editor he knows or has worked with before, the query might involve just a phone call. For a new editor or publication, he'll send a letter with a detailed but brief summary of the idea, along with copies of similar articles that he's published. In either case, he must have a very clear and specific idea of the story he wants to write.

Joseph explains that a freelancer's life goes through cycles. He describes periods of waiting for work followed by frantic episodes of meeting deadlines. A query might go unanswered for months, but once an editor finally decides he or she wants the work, it could be on a very short deadline. A few years ago Joseph had enough time to go on a two-week vacation, but returned home to find six contracts, all due in a month.

He feels that freelance writing is what you make it, explaining that you can be as busy (and successful) as you want to be. After all his experience, he is still learning to pace himself when it comes to getting work, and he still thinks that he could be doing twice as much writing (but at the risk of producing lower-quality work than he demands of himself). Despite this, however, he works a twelve-hour day, including writing, research, and interviewing.

The Upsides and Downsides

Aside from the thrill of seeing his name in print, Joseph says the best part of the job is the freedom of working for himself. "Of course," he explains, "I don't work for myself, I work for magazines and newspapers and editors, but each job has a different boss, and I know if I have a bad experience with one boss, I need not work for him or her again."

The negative side of the job is waiting—waiting for an assignment, and then waiting for the paycheck. Joseph also acknowledges the reality that being a freelance writer involves other work as well. He must keep track of his submissions, billing, and expenses, which can be tiring and overwhelming at times.

The work can also get lonely. He spends most of his time in his office, talking to himself in front of a computer screen. And there are times when it's necessary to convince friends and family that he is actually working even though he's home, and they must respect that.

Earnings

Joseph points out that someone just starting out can expect to earn very little, if anything. Most freelance writers do the work part-time, and often they don't get paid at all. But this is part of gaining experience and establishing yourself in the business.

"Once your reputation and skill warrant it, a freelance feature writer can expect to find widely varying pay rates," Joseph says. "Everything from five cents to $1 a word is typical (and some lower than that), while the big, national magazines will pay thousands of dollars an article. But that's a tough group to join."

Advice from a Professional

Joseph's first bit of advice is to love language and writing. He doesn't agree with writers who say they love having written, but hate writing—if you enjoy every part of the process, sitting in front of the computer or typewriter or notepad, you'll never suffer from writer's block.

To be a successful article writer, he believes that you should first be an article reader. Be aware of styles of writing. Read voraciously, and devour facts. It might be helpful to keep a journal where you can jot down observations of people and places. Learn how to put those observations on paper; it's called finding your voice. Writer and teacher Lary Bloom says that voice, the personal voice of the writer, is the most important part of any story; that is, what you yourself add to the article. Remember that only you can tell the story you are telling.

Joseph recommends finding a discussion group at your library or local bookstore, or even online, where you can talk about your daily encounters. Learn to listen. Contact your local newspaper, your church, any clubs you belong to, and local businesses to see if they have newsletters you can write for.

In summary, Joseph says, "The more words you put in print, the better your words get. And most importantly, never give up! I've been very lucky, being as successful as I've been in such a short time. Some writers take several years of hard work before they see real success. It can be very discouraging, but it's also very rewarding."

BARBARA STAHURA

Freelance Writer

Barbara Stahura started her freelance writing business, called Word Worker, in 1994. When she moved to Arizona five years later, she changed the name of the business to Clariti Communications (clariticom.com), which offers such writing-related services as feature article and book writing, copywriting, editing, copyediting, proofreading, and class and workshop facilitation.

Her most recent work has appeared in the publications *Science and Spirit*, *Science of Mind*, *Spirituality and Health*, and *The Progressive* magazine.

Getting Started

Barbara describes herself as a self-taught writer who has honed her skill at various workshops, such as the Iowa Writers' Workshop, the International

Women's Writing Guild annual conference at Skidmore College, and Rope Walk in New Harmony, Indiana. She also reads a great deal about writing.

Although she'd always said she wanted to be a writer, Barbara didn't pursue it until her midthirties, when she applied for a public information writing job with a utility company. She was hired (more for her management experience, since she didn't have any professional writing experience), and wrote everything from the company news magazine to bill inserts. Six years later, tired of the corporate world, she decided to try freelancing.

Barbara found her first clients through her connections with the utility company. She was also fortunate to connect with several local publishers and editors for whom she still writes. Her business has taken off from these beginnings.

Her first publication was an essay called "Fearless Self-Employment," originally published in *Science of Mind* magazine. In this piece Barbara describes how she made the decision to leave corporate life, which she says was killing her emotionally and spiritually.

The Realities of the Work

Barbara says that her duties are to write on various subjects in the style required by the project. Fortunately, she finds most of the things she writes about are interesting—or else she's able to work up some interest once she learns about the subject. Her natural curiosity helps in this area.

She says that marketing is her least favorite part of freelancing, although it's probably the most important. She's not as disciplined about it as she feels she should be, and she doesn't have a specific schedule for marketing as some writers do.

In terms of the workload, Barbara describes the job as "feast or famine." She works at home, which she enjoys for the freedom and independence it allows. On the other hand, since she lives alone it can be isolating.

She enjoys being able to write about a variety of subjects. Barbara describes herself as a generalist, so she doesn't usually specialize in any particular subject. Her work has covered such topics as Y2K, high-end fountain pens, jewelry design, microloans, meditation, various artists, archaeological finds, some travel experiences, local and regional entertainment and culture events, and a few computer-related issues. Her work has been published locally, regionally, nationally, and internationally. She has also written several books for a small local publisher: a history of the Indiana Farm Bureau, two county histories, and several histories of military units.

For two years, Barbara was editor of the *Indiana Journal of Commerce and Industry*. She began writing for the same publisher on other publications in the early 1990s, when she was still working at the utility. The journal approached her in 1997, when they were looking for an editor, and she took them on as another client.

She is a senior writer for a Florida publisher who often contacts her with assignments. In addition, she can also suggest her own topics and provides proofreading and copyediting services to the publisher as well.

Early in her freelance career, Barbara did a lot of writing for local businesses, mainly newsletters and brochures. Since this is the type of writing she enjoys least, she is happy to have been able to drop most of it now that other types of work have picked up. (See Chapter 9 for more information on newsletter writing.)

Barbara is also a radio essayist for the local NPR affiliate, writing and recording very short essays that are broadcast during *Morning Edition*. There's no pay for this, but she enjoys having her essays on the radio and considers the positive feedback she's heard from people to be the payoff.

She says it's hard to describe a typical day, because some days are spent on research, appointments, and interviews, while others are devoted to writing. Barbara feels that one of the greatest advantages to being a free-lancer is the ability to set her own schedule and to take time off when she needs or wants to. One of the things she liked least about corporate life was the need to work according to someone else's schedule. Being on her own, she can go to the gym in the morning and work later in the day, and then continue working into the evening if she wants to.

Barbara estimates that she works between forty and sixty hours a week, generally working as many hours in a day as is necessary. Since she lives alone, it's easy to spend a lot of time working, but she tries to keep a balance between work and leisure. "I'm fairly disciplined," she says. "Impending starvation is a good motivator, but I try not to be too hard on myself. I take Brenda Ueland's advice in *If You Want to Write*. She says we have to give ourselves time to 'moodle,' which means taking time to relax and play and just not think about much of anything, if we are to be able to recharge ourselves and our creativity."

The Upsides and Downsides

What Barbara likes most about her work is the freedom to explore and write about subjects that interest her. The freedom to set her own schedule is also near the top of the list. She enjoys the opportunity to meet and interview interesting people she otherwise wouldn't have the opportunity to talk with.

Barbara feels that being a freelancer has broadened her horizons and experience in a way no other job could have done, which is part of the reason she decided to do it. The longer she works, the more she learns to trust her intuition about which jobs will be good for her and which will not. She has quit or turned down jobs because they would have been too stressful or boring or didn't fit into her plans. She even quit an editing job that represented 40 percent of her income because the management became so dysfunctional that she could no longer deal with them honorably. She is pleased that so far, she hasn't made a bad decision in that regard.

The only thing Barbara dislikes about the job is the need to market herself. She says it's the hardest and least interesting thing she has to do, although it's the most important. She feels fortunate that many long-term clients whom she enjoys working with respect her work, and that new work comes along when she needs it.

Earnings

Before she began freelancing, Barbara read that the average freelance writer makes $7,000 a year. She believed she could do better than that and is happy to say that she has. Although her annual income fluctuates, she has had the experience of earning more in one year than she ever did in corporate life, which was $35,000. "My freelance income has always been over $25,000, which is not too bad in this part of the country," she says. "As I gain more experience, I keep making more, for which I'm grateful."

Advice from a Professional

Barbara says that it's hard for her to offer advice to anyone who wants to be a freelance writer because she's never followed the advice in the writing magazines, however worthwhile it is. She says, "Because I was so desperate to get out of corporate life, I just jumped off the cliff. Then I worked like a dog and also learned to trust my intuition. I think I'm fortunate in that I did so well right off the bat. Maybe that comes from the contentment I feel with this kind of work."

Barbara acknowledges that there have been times of uncertainty, but she credits her own commitment and the support of family and friends with helping her to continue on her path and to succeed. She recommends that any aspiring freelancer have some degree of this essential and priceless support. She also says, "Another thing that keeps me going is my absolute refusal to ever have a 'real' job again. Maybe that kind of stubbornness will serve someone else well, too."

The qualities that Barbara feels every freelance writer needs are persistence, determination, discipline, patience, willingness to learn, and the ability to handle rejection. You must also be willing to keep improving your skills, and never rest on your past accomplishments. She says that while this may be true for any job, freelancing doesn't allow you to coast for very long. "You must be willing to give up some financial reward, at least in the beginning, and be prepared to live on less for a time," Barbara says. "For me, this was something I did willingly, given that my last corporate job that paid well was stressful beyond words. The rewards for me have gone far beyond financial. Being a freelancer has given me the opportunity and freedom to begin finding myself, something that never would have been possible for me in a corporate setting."

TANYA LOCHRIDGE
Freelace Medical/Health-Care Writer

Tanya Lochridge writes medical/health-care magazine articles, patient education materials, and presentation materials primarily for the consumer/patient audience. In addition, she prepares annual reports for managed-care organizations and pharmaceutical companies. Her clients include pharmaceutical companies, managed-care organizations, magazines, websites, medical associations, nonprofit associations, and hospitals. She has been freelancing since 1984.

Getting Started

Tanya always knew she wanted to be a writer, but she wasn't sure she'd be able to make a living at it. After teaching for several years, she realized that this wasn't the right profession for her, and she found a job at a pharmaceutical company in Southern California. She spent a year working in market research, where she designed, implemented, and wrote various market-research studies. This made her realize that she could make a living by writing.

While working in market research, Tanya began talking with copywriters and other writers to learn what was required for their job and how they reached their positions. She says that all of her work from that point in some way led to her current success as a freelancer. For several years she worked in various aspects of the pharmaceutical industry, such as sales, marketing, and education. She credits this experience with providing a much broader background than that of most writers, thereby giving her a slight edge in the market.

The Realities of the Work

Tanya acknowledges that although freelance writing has many positives and negatives, for her the positives far outweigh any negative aspects. Her day begins about 10:00 or 11:00 A.M. when she checks e-mail for assignment updates, and then writes until about 3:00 in the afternoon, taking short breaks to stretch. At 3:00 she return calls, checks with editors or directors on assignments, and then returns to writing until about 9:00 in the evening (although some night she writes until 2:00 or 3:00 in the morning, depending on the work flow).

This is the schedule she keeps when there is plenty of work in the pipeline. If assignments begin to slow down, she sends out promo materials to existing clients and potential new clients. So, basically she is either working on a specific assignment or working on promotion and marketing. Tanya estimates that when she is working on a project, 80 percent of her time is spent researching the topic, and the remaining 20 percent is spent writing. She says, "Sometimes, to clear my head, I grab the dog and head for the park. What appears to be play to the innocent passerby is really a time for structuring and solving problems in a current assignment."

The Upsides and Downsides

Tanya likes many things about working as a freelancer. One is the ability to use her talents to help consumers and patients who have health concerns, knowing that she can possibly have an effect on someone's life, because the person took the time to read the material she produced, and then sought medical advice. She enjoys the freedom to be casual at work, with her dog keeping her company, working into the wee hours of the morning if she wants to. She also likes the freedom to pick and choose the projects she works on.

What Tanya likes least is being the bill collector. Although some clients pay invoices promptly, others make her chase after her money. However, over the years this has become less of a problem, as she's been able to weed out the slow payers by turning down their assignments.

Sometimes she finds it too easy to work around the clock, which can throw her life out of balance. But she does this because as a freelancer, she wants to take all assignments when they come, because there is no guarantee that they will come again next month. She lives on a strict budget, no matter how much she earns in a month.

Earnings

Tanya reports that her annual earnings generally exceed $125,000. She cautions, however, that she's been doing this work for many years, and works in a specialty area in which few writers succeed.

"It takes a certain skill to be able to take 'medicalese' and make it consumer-friendly without talking down to the reader," she says. "I believe I could be earning more after all these years, but I am at a point in my life where I am trying to strike a balance between my work and my personal life."

Advice from a Professional

Tanya says that to succeed as a freelancer, you must first and foremost be a good writer. She believes that part of being a great writer is being an avid reader, and advises that you read anything you can that fits into the category you are interested in, as well as all the stuff you can that just gives you joy.

She feels that while education opens the door, once you're working you must prove yourself, again and again. It takes a while to establish a reputation in an industry, so patience and persistence are two important qualities. You also need good researching skills, and you must learn to use rejection constructively to improve your skills.

Tanya recommends developing a promotional package that lists your education, clients, and skills and that includes samples of your work. If you are starting out and don't have previous work, write some samples that can be included. Keep in mind that it might take more than one promo package to get the job. She suggests doing regular mailings every few weeks (she still mails once a month to all clients and includes samples of projects recently completed).

Another piece of advice is to work in-house with a company or agency for a while, which lends more credibility to your credentials.

Always continue to learn and upgrade your skills. For example, Tanya started by writing brochures, added newsletters and magazine articles, and now writes content for the Web as well. Each of these requires a slightly different set of skills, so it's best to stay current. Never, ever miss a deadline—that will be your undoing. Everything you did before will be forgotten and the missed deadline will long be remembered.

Tanya warns that if you want to freelance because you think it is easier than working in an office, you should reconsider your decision. Most freelancers work in a vacuum, without the luxury of bouncing ideas off colleagues or just complaining to colleagues about a current project, which can be a relief at times.

As a freelance writer, you not only complete projects for clients, you also have to complete projects for yourself on a regular basis. There are no paid holidays, paid vacation, paid sick days. Every day you must get up and write.

SUZANNE CASEY
Freelance Reporter and Stringer

Suzanne Casey is a freelance reporter and stringer for Central Record Publications, which puts out several local weeklies and monthlies in New Jersey. She also writes feature stories for various publications. She has been writing since 1990.

Getting Started

Suzanne believes that writing chose her. She has always kept journals and written stories, and early in her business career she started writing for newsletters and business trade journals because she had something to contribute. She describes getting published as a powerful motivator to keep going.

She got her start by responding to a request for articles in a trade publication that she subscribed to. She wrote a short article on recycling in an office environment, and seeing it published gave her the motivation and courage to try again.

Several years later, after the birth of her second child, Suzanne decided to stay at home and combine her freelance writing with a business support service. With this combination of services and skills, she is now financially back to the point where she was before becoming home-based.

She got her current job because a friend who was writing feature stories for a monthly publication gave the editor her name as a possible writer for future assignments. That first assignment has led to a hectic schedule of deadlines for more than four publications under their banner. Suzanne says that the work has continued to strengthen her confidence to submit to different (and bigger) publications with a further reach.

The Realities of the Work

A stringer is basically a part-time or freelance correspondent for a news publication, often employed by community newspapers or city dailies that don't have enough staff reporters to handle all the stories they need. Stringers cover everything from school-board meetings to lower-interest sporting events to breaking spot news. Suzanne feels that it's a good way for a beginner to break into the field, as long as you don't mind covering town and school meetings or sporting events.

Suzanne is fortunate to have both a stringer and freelance relationship with the papers she works for. For example, she covers zoning and planning meetings as a stringer and usually reports on variances and uses. After hearing month after month about the plans for all the businesses that were coming into town, she used the information to write a freelance business-page story that covered the explosive commercial growth in a town following its residential boom.

Her duties include research on the Internet and at libraries. She conducts interviews on the phone or in person, and then writes the story. She loves the process, even when the interviewee is tough: either cautious to the point of not talking or doesn't know what to say beyond the one-word response. She gets to meet really wonderful people who do interesting things, and she learns about things she wouldn't otherwise know about.

Suzanne's articles have ranged from straight news reporting (municipal, school, business) to features (lifestyles, people profiles, arts and entertainment), to advertorials, to theater reviews, to business features. She also occasionally writes copy for business material (brochures and marketing pieces).

While the majority of her stories are assignments, she also has some supportive editors who encourage her ideas and welcome her suggestions for stories. At this point in her career, it's rare not to have a story idea accepted by one of her editors.

Suzanne recalls a newspaper writer/Pulitzer winner who told her, "You have to move the furniture around. E verybody has a story to tell; it's up to you as a writer to find it." She has taken these words as inspiration for finding what may not be obvious at first glance.

She says that the key is to know the needs of your editor or publication, and stresses the importance of knowing the market. When she finds an interesting topic, she discusses it with the editor of that section; if it doesn't fit, he or she might suggest where it would work better.

Suzanne has reached the point where she can explore ideas with her editors, who are receptive to her input. She also keeps index cards with subject headings and a list of publications, so that if an idea comes up she can check who might be interested in it.

She acknowledges that some days can be difficult because she has young children and wants to accommodate their needs as much as her schedule will allow. Although her days are somewhat flexible, allowing her to attend school functions when needed or take a walk or bike ride, she stresses the importance of sticking to a quasi-schedule of work. Structure and a daily plan are vital to meeting deadlines, and if she misses a day because her children need her, then she'll work later at night to make up the lost time.

"Don't get me wrong, there are days when I enjoy doing nothing but enjoying my family," Suzanne says. "But small children are the great unknown in the mix. It's really important to have backup babysitters, a quiet room to duck into when someone starts wailing unexpectedly, or a mute button on your phone. My kids know that when I'm on the phone, they're not to interrupt me when my hand goes up (except for emergencies). This took some training."

Suzanne usually makes her interview calls first thing in the morning, followed by writing. She tries to work on an average of one to two stories a day, which gives her the rest of the day for callbacks and meetings. She takes a lunch break and a play break for her daughter, and sometimes they go to the library together or work on projects at the kitchen table. She writes more at night, after her children are in bed. This is also when she does her Internet research.

Sometimes she has to cover meetings at night (anywhere from a half hour to three hours, one to two per week), or events (shows, happenings, and so forth). Some events are great for taking family or friends to get feedback.

The Upsides and Downsides

"I love the work," Suzanne says. "On 99 percent of my interviews, the people and the things they do are so very interesting. I am constantly learning. And amazingly, one thing always seems to lead to another, whether it is another story idea or a new contact. Getting the scoop or piece of information that no one else has always feels good."

What she likes least is interviewing people who don't want to be interviewed, asking the hard questions, finding out that someone held out some vital piece of information for her story and getting blindsided on it, struggling to find the right angle for the story, and trying to meet deadlines when things are falling apart around her.

Earnings

Suzanne is paid by the story. In the early days of her career, she generally earned from $25 to a couple of hundred dollars, based on the publication. Some newspapers pay only $25 to $35 per story, but adding a sidebar or photos can double the amount. Since she usually has several projects going simultaneously, she receives various payment amounts.

"The catch for me is my children," Suzanne says. "If I had all day to freely dedicate to my craft, I would be able to increase my income. Because I choose to make my kids my priority, sometimes the writing has to wait.

"I think anyone just starting out as a freelancer should expect to need a cushion for at least a year, maybe more. I think it depends on the time you expect to devote to your writing and, of course, whether a person is any good. I was lucky to have my husband as a strong positive support factor in my career choices. It was a struggle at first, but it has definitely paid off."

Advice from a Professional

Suzanne's main bit of advice is to keep writing. "Just keep plugging and making contacts," she says. "All it takes is one of those contacts to get you published and the rest will fall in line because your confidence and motivation are built up with each one. And with every year you get better and better, and the better assignments come with that."

THREE HELPFUL TIPS

There are a few things you can do to further your career as a freelance writer for newspapers and magazines. Here are three tips to get you started.

• Be sure that you've thoroughly researched your article and that your writing is polished and professional.

• Submit professional query letters and manuscripts. Follow the submission requirements of the publication.

• Make sure you're submitting your work to the right publication. A magazine that publishes articles about healthy low-fat cooking won't publish your piece on developing the ultimate recipe for fudge brownies.

C H A P T E R

5

STAFF WRITERS AND REPORTERS

"Writing is the only profession where no one considers you ridiculous
if you earn no money."

–Jules Renard

In the last chapter, you read that many publications print articles written
by freelancers. In addition to these writers, however, most newspapers and
magazines hire full-time staff writers and reporters and depend on them
to fill the pages with articles or news reports.

Staff writers and reporters don't usually have the luxury of setting their
own hours the way freelancers do, and most are expected to come into
the office every day. They are given article assignments to research and
write, or stories to cover, and they often work with an editor to develop
ideas.

While freelancers have the advantage of proposing their own story ideas,
staff writers and reporters generally have more job security and always
know when their next paycheck will arrive. Freelancers trade job security
and regular pay for their independence.

As in any aspect of writing, full-time magazine writers and newspaper
reporters have to produce high-quality work. They have editors to report
to and deadlines to meet.

WRITING FOR MAGAZINES

Visit any bookstore or newsstand and you'll see hundreds of magazines covering a variety of topics—from cooking and vacations to spirituality and parenting. There are also many you won't see there, the hundreds of trade journals and magazines written for businesses, industries, and professional workers in as many different careers. These publications all offer information on diverse subjects to their equally diverse readership. They are filled with articles and profiles, interviews and editorials, letters and advice, as well as pages and pages of advertisements. But without writers there would be nothing but advertisements between their covers—and even those are produced by writers!

Working Conditions

Writers hold more than 400,000 jobs throughout the United States and Canada, with nearly a third of salaried writers working for magazines and newspapers. Jobs with major magazines are concentrated in New York, Chicago, Los Angeles, Boston, Philadelphia, San Francisco, Washington, D.C., Toronto, and Vancouver.

After receiving an assignment, a staff writer gathers information through personal observation, library research, and interviews. The search for information sometimes requires travel and visits to diverse settings, such as factories, offices, laboratories, ballparks, or theaters, or it may involve only telephone interviews and research.

The workweek usually runs thirty-five to forty hours. Writers who prepare morning or weekend publications and broadcasts work nights and/or weekends. Many writers work overtime to meet deadlines or to cover late-developing stories, and deadlines are often part of the daily routine.

Job Requirements

In general, you'll need a college degree to qualify for a position as a staff writer. Although some employers look for a broad liberal arts background, most prefer to hire applicants with degrees in communications, journalism, or English. It's also a good idea to take courses in another area as well, either to qualify yourself as a writer specializing in that field or to enter that field if you are unable to get a job in writing.

As with any area of writing, you must be able to express ideas clearly and logically and should love to write. The qualities of creativity, curiosity, self-motivation, and perseverance will also serve you well. For some jobs, the ability to concentrate amid confusion and to work under pressure is essential. A growing number of publications look for writers who are familiar with electronic publishing, graphics, and video production equipment. Online magazines require knowledge of computer software used to combine online text with graphics, audio, video, and 3D animation.

You can gain valuable (but sometimes unpaid) experience writing for high school and college newspapers, literary magazines, and community newspapers and radio and television stations. Many magazines offer internships to students, during which they write short pieces, conduct research and interviews, and learn about the publishing business.

You might start out as an editorial assistant, displaying your talents on the job and winning a promotion. But to get a full-time, permanent position or regular assignments from a publication, you'll need a successful track record and a portfolio of published clips showcasing your best work.

The Job Outlook

Employment of staff writers for magazines is expected to increase as demand grows for these publications over the next decade. Magazines and other periodicals increasingly are developing market niches, appealing to readers with special interests. In addition, the growing number of online publications and services will continue to create job opportunities for writers.

Potential Earnings

According to the most recently available information from the Bureau of Labor Statistics, in 2004 median annual earnings for salaried writers were $44,350; the majority earned between $31,720 and $62,930. The lowest 10 percent earned less than $23,330, and the highest 10 percent earned more than $91,260.

As shown in Chapter 4, salaries for writers are seldom glamorous. But full-time staff writers have the advantage of employment benefits such as health insurance, sick leave, and vacation time. Freelancers have to foot the bill for these perks themselves.

WRITING FOR NEWSPAPERS, TELEVISION, AND RADIO

Do you like being on top of things, always knowing what's going on around you? If so, a job working for a newspaper might be the right career choice for you. Reporters, editors, and photojournalists are assigned to a variety of stories, from the exciting and dangerous to the offbeat and tame.

Those with an adventurous nature might relish the idea of being in the thick of a downtown riot or chasing fire engines to the scene of a car wreck. Others might find themselves on the front line in a war zone or witnessing flood rescues or criminal activity.

For the less adventurous, there are specialized fields to cover such as health and medicine, fashion and food, and arts and entertainment.

The departments within newspapers vary from location to location, but most include at least some, if not all, of the following sections:

Art	Health
Entertainment	International News
Business	Lifestyles/Features
Books	Local News
Consumer Affairs	National News
The Courts	Religion
Crime Desk	Science
Education	Social Events
Fashion	Sports
Finance	State News
Food	Travel
Foreign Affairs	Weather

In covering a story, reporters investigate leads and news tips, look at documents, observe on the scene, and interview people. They organize the material, determine their focus or emphasis, and write the story. Many use notebook computers to take notes and write their stories, and then submit them electronically to their offices. In some cases, newswriters write the story from information collected and submitted by the reporter.

General assignment reporters cover such events as a political rally, the visit of a celebrity, or a company going out of business. Those who work for large newspapers and for broadcast media are usually assigned to report about specific news categories, such as crime or education. Some reporters specialize in fields such as health, politics, foreign affairs, sports, theater, consumer affairs, social events, science, business, and religion. Investigative reporters cover stories that take many days or weeks of information gathering. News correspondents are stationed in other locations and report on news occurring in large U.S., Canadian, or foreign cities.

Reporters on small publications cover all aspects of the news and generally perform all related duties—they take photographs, write headlines, lay out pages, edit wire-service copy, and write editorials. They may also solicit advertisements, sell subscriptions, and perform general office work.

Newswriters prepare items for newspapers or news broadcasts based on information supplied by reporters or wire services. Columnists analyze news and write commentaries based on personal knowledge and experience. Editorial writers write comments to stimulate or mold public opinion in accordance with their publication's viewpoint. Columnists and editorial writers are able to take sides on issues, be subjective, and express their opinions, while other newswriters must be objective and neutral in their coverage.

Working Conditions

The work of news analysts, reporters, and correspondents is usually hectic. They are under great pressure to meet deadlines, and broadcasts are sometimes aired with little or no time for preparation. Some work in comfortable, private offices; others work in large rooms filled with the noise of keyboards and computer printers, as well as the sounds of other reporters. The work can also be dangerous for those covering wars, political uprisings, and natural disasters.

Working hours vary. Reporters on morning papers often work from late afternoon until midnight. Radio and television reporters usually are assigned to a day or evening shift. Regardless of their assigned shift, reporters sometimes have to change their hours to meet a deadline or to follow late-breaking developments. Their work demands long hours, irregular schedules, and some travel.

Job Requirements

Most employers prefer applicants with a bachelor's degree in journalism, but some hire graduates with other majors. They look for experience on school newspapers or broadcasting stations as well as internships with news organizations. Large city newspapers and stations may also prefer candidates with a degree in a subject-matter specialty, such as economics, political science, or business. In addition, large newspapers require a minimum of three to five years' experience as a reporter.

You can find programs in journalism, communications, and related fields at more than 1,200 institutions in the United States and Canada. In 2004, 104 of these were accredited by the Accrediting Council on Education in Journalism and Mass Communications. About three-fourths of the courses in a typical curriculum are in liberal arts; the remaining journalism courses include introductory mass media, basic reporting and copyediting, history of journalism, and press law and ethics.

Most students planning newspaper careers usually specialize in news-editorial journalism. If you are planning a career in new media, such as online newspapers, you will need both traditional and new journalism skills. To create a story for multimedia presentation, you must know how to use computer software to combine online story text with graphics, audio and video elements, and even 3D animation.

Some schools offer master's degrees and Ph.D.s in journalism. Some graduate programs are intended primarily as preparation for news careers, while others will prepare you for a career as a journalism teacher, researcher and theorist, or advertising and public relations worker.

Your high school courses in English, journalism, and social studies will provide a good foundation for college programs. Useful college-level liberal-arts courses include English with an emphasis on writing, sociology, political science, economics, history, and psychology. Courses in computer science, business, and speech are helpful as well, and you might need fluency in a foreign language for some jobs.

To work as a reporter, you'll need good word-processing skills, and computer graphics and desktop publishing skills are also important. Experience on high school and college newspapers and broadcasting stations, community papers, and armed forces publications helps, as does any experience in a part-time or summer job or an internship with a news organization. The Dow Jones Newspaper Fund and newspapers, magazines, and broadcast news organizations offer summer reporting and editing internships (see Appendix A for more information). And any experience you've gained as a stringer, a part-time reporter who is paid only for stories printed, is another plus.

To be a successful reporter, you must be dedicated to providing accurate and impartial news. A "nose for news," persistence, initiative, poise, resourcefulness, a good memory, and physical stamina are important, as is the emotional stability to deal with pressing deadlines, irregular hours, and dangerous assignments. You must be able to feel at ease in unfamiliar places and with a variety of people.

Most reporters start at small publications or broadcast stations as general assignment reporters or copyeditors. Large publications and stations don't hire many recent graduates; they generally require reporters to have several years of experience.

As a beginning reporter, you'll cover court proceedings and civic and club meetings, summarize speeches, and write obituaries. With experience, you'll move on to more difficult assignments, cover an assigned beat, or specialize in a particular field.

After you've gained experience, you may be able to advance by moving to a larger paper. Some experienced reporters become columnists, correspondents, writers, announcers, or public relations specialists. Others become editors in print journalism or program managers in broadcast journalism, who supervise reporters. Some eventually become broadcasting or publications industry managers.

Getting Ahead

Reporters have to be prepared to move to where the jobs are. You could waste a lot of time waiting for that perfect position to open up at your hometown paper. You don't want to have six different jobs in three years, but you should stay at a paper only long enough to utilize everything it has to offer.

And while on the job, be on the lookout for a mentor. Look to someone who is older and more experienced, someone you can trust and who will take your career seriously. A mentor can be invaluable in helping to analyze mistakes so that you don't repeat them. And if you go to him or her with questions first, you can avoid many mistakes altogether.

The Job Outlook

Competition is expected to be keen for jobs on large metropolitan and national newspapers, broadcast stations and networks, and magazines through 2014. Most opportunities will be with small-town and suburban newspapers and radio and television stations. Talented writers who can handle highly specialized scientific or technical subjects have an advantage. Also, newspapers increasingly are hiring stringers and freelancers.

For several reasons, employment of news analysts, reporters, and correspondents is expected to increase by no more than 8 percent through the year 2014. Consolidation and convergence is likely to continue in the publishing and broadcasting industries. As a result, companies will be better able to allocate their news analysts, reporters, and correspondents to cover news stories. Constantly improving technology also is allowing workers to do their jobs more efficiently, another factor that will limit the number of workers needed to cover a story or certain type of news.

The continued demand for news will create some job opportunities, however. For example, some job growth will most likely occur in newer media areas, such as online newspapers and magazines. Job openings also will result from the need to replace workers who leave their occupations permanently; some news analysts, reporters, and correspondents find the work too stressful and hectic or do not like the lifestyle, and transfer to other occupations.

Potential Earnings

Salaries for news analysts, reporters, and correspondents vary widely. In 2004 these professionals had median annual earnings of $31,320. Most earned between $22,900 and $47,860, but the lowest 10 percent earned less than $18,470, and the highest 10 percent earned more than $68,250.

Median annual earnings of broadcast news analysts were $36,980 in 2004, with the majority earning between $25,560 and $68,440. While most earned between $25,560 and $68,440, the lowest paid earned less than $19,040 and the highest paid earned more than $122,800.

The Newspaper Guild negotiates reporters' wages with newspapers, from starting salaries to the highest earnings, which take effect after three to six years of employment. Variations in salary will occur depending on the geographic region in which you work. Salaries are higher in cities such as New York and Washington, but the cost of living is also much higher.

FIRSTHAND ACCOUNTS

Two reporters have shared their stories with us; read the accounts of their very different careers to gain some insight into this exciting field.

ANNE MARIE KING-JAKUBIAK
Reporter

Anne Marie King-Jakubiak worked for many years as a journalist with a small-town newspaper in Michigan. She did some investigative reporting and wrote features, movie and theater reviews, and commentaries. She still writes freelance articles and newsletters, but she is concentrating on writing contemporary and historical romances.

She received a bachelor of arts in communication with a double major in journalism and English from Madonna University in Livonia, Michigan.

Getting Started

Anne Marie says that she was always interested in writing and was still in grade school when her first poem was published and she began winning writing contests. She has always kept a journal in which she recorded impressions of people who were important in her life. As a child, she begged her grandmother to tell stories about her early life, and she loved to hear about her great-grandmother's experiences during the Civil War era.

In high school she took journalism courses and worked on the school paper. She got her first job by walking into a small-town newspaper office and showing her portfolio of stories, including freelance, high school newspaper, and college newspaper. The newspaper needed help, and Anne Marie needed professional experience.

The Realities of the Work

Anne Marie admits that being a newspaper reporter was not much fun for her, mainly because of the high stress imposed by editors. It was also a round-the-clock job. There were times when she would get home only to be called out again on an assignment, which was difficult for a single parent.

Writing movie and theater critiques was fun, though, because Anne Marie would get two tickets to the screening or performance and could bring a friend or one of her children.

Her one good experience with an editor was while she was working as an investigative reporter. During this time, Anne Marie's work usually led to a front page, five- or six-page series. For example, while reporting a series on malpractice, her first story was on the attorneys' point of view, followed by those of the insurance companies, physicians, and patients, with a final story that tied the series together. As one question led to another, Anne Marie received confidential documents from friends who worked for lawyers and insurance companies, as well as doctors she had befriended.

While reporting a story on illegal dumping, she received death threats at work and at home, demanding that she drop the story. Because she was writing for a small newspaper, Anne Marie was surprised that anyone really cared about the story, having forgotten that organized crime was behind the dumping. Her editor remembered, however, and immediately gave the story to a male reporter and assigned Anne Marie to writing feature stories. The editor told her that when her youngest child reached eighteen she could go back to investigative work, but Anne Marie found that she lost interest in reporting after working on features for a couple of years.

She says that features can be fun, such as a Valentine's Day story she wrote about how couples met and what their first date was like. On the other hand, she acknowledges that they can be intrusive, as with a story about a family tragedy such as a house fire or a child who has been killed. It is difficult and painful for people to answer questions under these circumstances, and Anne Marie felt that she was intruding on private grief. At these times, she saw the need to be sensitive and very careful with quotes.

A good deal of the job is routine. A lot of the work involves getting background, looking into history, and visiting libraries. A newspaper writer must be accurate and quick—all facts must be verifiable, and deadlines can't be ignored.

Anne Marie says that conducting interviews can be interesting if a reporter is prepared. With the proper research and a short list of questions to ask or items to cover, the interview should flow naturally. After introducing herself and stating what she was after, she would ask the first question and give the interviewee time to answer. If the person paused or hesitated, she wouldn't speak until the person had finished—this way the person often supplied more information than she'd expected, because the silence made him or her nervous.

Anne Marie spent a lot of time on the phone to sources and contacts and a lot of time in libraries tracking down background and other information. Contacts and private sources are important because a human voice telling about an experience with emotion can add a lot to a story. Facial expressions and body language are also important. On the phone, the joy or disapproval you hear in a voice can mean a lot.

The Upsides and Downsides

On the positive side, Anne Marie loved the excitement of meeting new people and meeting famous people and trying to figure out what makes them tick. She also enjoyed digging deep behind the stories and discovering the bad guys.

What she disliked were the long hours and being called out just when she was involved with her kids. She hated canceling plans at the last minute to follow a story or a lead, and she says that she still can't go to a movie or play or read a book without critiquing it.

Advice from a Professional

Anne Marie suggests befriending your contacts, who can become your best sources and lead to other important sources in the future. You have to love the job and have the time to devote to it. A natural curiosity and quick mind are essential to doing a good job.

She also recommends that you be prepared for anything, and keep your opinions to yourself. Watch your own facial expressions and body language, and be friendly with everyone. You never know if someone you meet will in the future become a source, story, or contact.

Obviously, she adds, you must also be able to write well and keep a fast pace.

Anne Marie thinks that high school journalism courses are important, and that keeping a journal will strengthen your writing skills and curiosity. You should also take college courses, and a bachelor's degree is highly recommended. A master's degree isn't required for reporting jobs, but it will help if you plan on teaching.

Anne Marie recommends keeping a portfolio of your work. Starting your career at a small newspaper, perhaps while you are in college, is a good beginning. Although it might seem mundane because you'll probably be reporting on town meetings at first, it will give you good experience.

Finally, Anne Marie says, "Keep an even temper, and work hard. Be persistent. Get out of the job if you find yourself losing compassion and becoming too cynical. Remember, someone who is in the grips of a tragedy needs to be treated with kid gloves and not be exploited."

ROD STAFFORD HAGWOOD
Fashion Writer/Editor

Rod Stafford Hagwood started freelance writing in college, and in 1990 he moved directly from an internship into his present job as fashion editor at the *Fort Lauderdale Sun-Sentinel*.

Getting Started

Although his high school guidance counselor suggested that he consider studying law, Rod wasn't interested in pursuing that path. He wanted to do something less restrictive, but he wasn't sure he could make a living from his interest in writing.

Rod started freelancing for local papers while he was in college. He wrote entertainment pieces and was lucky enough to meet people who helped him to arrange interviews with celebrities he wouldn't have been able to reach on his own. Some of his early interviews included Tom Cruise, Emilio Estevez, and Molly Ringwald.

By graduation, Rod had established an impressive portfolio of celebrity interviews and found a position with the Gannett Company, parent company of more than ninety daily newspapers, including *USA Today*. He was offered an internship at the *Arkansas Gazette* that would lead to full-time employment within the company. While covering fund-raisers in Little Rock, he met Bill and Hillary Clinton, about whom he wrote many pieces. He wrote everything from classical music reviews to fashion and society pieces. He flew with the Blue Angels and attended country club debutante balls.

Rod learned of the job with the *Sun-Sentinel* through a *USA Today* fashion editor. Although he wasn't sure about the job, he decided to go to Fort Lauderdale for an interview and at least enjoy a weekend in Florida. Since he hadn't taken the job offer very seriously, he was unprepared for some of the questions posed. When asked what he would do as fashion editor, Rod improvised and described a fashion section that is funny and whimsical, as well as a bit naughty, and with a distinctive voice that would be recognizable as his. Apparently this was the right answer, and he was offered the job.

One of the factors that strongly influenced his decision to accept the position was advice from a fashion editor who told Rod that south Florida would be the next big place in fashion. As soon as he arrived, South Beach exploded into the public eye and he had plenty to write about.

What the Work Is Like

Rod's main responsibility is to produce the Sunday fashion page. He ensures that the art and photography meet the required standards and that the layout artist receives all the different elements in enough time to work with them. The actual writing involves phone calls and research. Rod covers trends in fashion, rather than writing stories on already famous models or designers.

The Upsides and Downsides

Rod likes the ability to set his own rules and explore anything that interests him. He can tell his boss he's heading for the mall, and that's perfectly acceptable. He can spend a day at the beach to see what swimsuits people are wearing—again, it's part of the job. He recently spent several days being pampered in upscale hair salons while researching an article on new hair products.

Rod says, "This is a wonderful kind of freedom, and it keeps you from becoming jaded and tired in your job. You'll never be bored. I can't even think of a downside."

Advice from a Professional

Rod advises that you need to be self-secure to succeed as a fashion writer, because the fashion industry includes many extremely insecure and difficult people. "I would have made a wonderful ambassador," he says. "You spend a lot of time trying to charm temperamental people.

"I think my parents taught me a wonderful lesson: you have to be the one to define who and what you are; don't let anyone else define you. Being black and a male and a fashion editor, you have to be secure. And if you have that kind of security, you are always in control, and you won't get upset by what other people do."

THREE HELPFUL TIPS

Here are three tips to keep in mind as you start your career as a staff writer:

• Try to get some published credits, either by submitting freelance articles to magazines and newspapers or by working as a volunteer or intern on a small paper. This will help you to gain good experience before applying for a staff job.

• Keep a portfolio of your work to show editors.

• Be realistic about getting that first staff job. It's quite likely that you'll start as an editorial assistant or proofreader before you're given the writing job you want.

CHAPTER

SCREENWRITING

"A screenwriter is a man who is being tortured to confess and has nothing to confess."
—Christopher Isherwood

"Take the money and run."
—Ernest Hemingway

You love movies and you've dreamed about seeing your name roll by on the credits as the person who wrote the screenplay.

If you've read Chapter 2, you've discovered how difficult it is to break into the world of print fiction. So maybe you're thinking that getting a screenplay produced will be easier. Think again! Although not impossible—thousands of screenplays are made into movies every year, and some by unknowns—the competition is fierce and the process is far more involved than writing and pitching a novel.

While book publishers do spend a lot of money on each book they publish, the figures are nowhere near what it takes to produce and distribute a movie. Considering that Julia Roberts and Johnny Depp each earn $20 million per picture, imagine how many other millions must be budgeted to cover the fees of other actors, the camera crew, the director, the producer, the writers, and people responsible for special effects, sound, lighting, location scouting, hair, wardrobe, makeup, travel, food, film, studio time, and so on. With so much money at stake, major film producers often prefer to work with big-name screenwriters who have built solid reputations and might even have an Oscar or two to their credit.

While all this might sound rather daunting, don't be discouraged. There's more than one route you can take, but you must know your craft, be dedicated and persistent, know the "tools of the trade," and know how to pitch your work. With this, and a little luck, you just might see your name on that screen.

THE TOOLS OF THE TRADE

Not only must you have a stellar screenplay, but as a screenwriter you must also know how to craft query letters, loglines, synopses, treatments, and outlines. Let's look at a definition of each.

Query Letter

Just as writers of novels, nonfiction books, and articles need to approach editors and agents with a query letter, so must screenwriters. The most effective query letter for a screenplay is one page, gives a brief overview of the premise, and provides information about you, the writer. For a sample query letter and an analysis of its important elements, see Figure 6.1.

Logline

A logline is a one- to two-sentence description of your premise. It can be used in person-to-person pitch sessions, in the body of your query letter as an opener to explain your story's premise, or in contests.

Synopsis

The synopsis is a one-page, single-spaced summary of your plot. This differs from a novel synopsis in that it's more of a *selling* tool than a *telling* tool.

Treatment

A treatment can be anywhere from three to fifteen double-spaced pages, describing every scene. Focus on the characters and their conflicts, using little or no dialogue.

Outline

Some studios might want to see a step outline, which describes each scene but uses only one line per scene.

SAMPLE QUERY LETTER

Screenwriter Christina Hamlett has provided an example of a query letter for her screenplay, *Everything but the Groom* (see Figure 6.1). Currently

Figure 6.1: Sample Query Letter

(On your letterhead with your phone number and e-mail address)

Date

Producer's Name
Studio Name
Address

(1) Dear Producer's Name,

(2) Your name was graciously provided to me by one of your fellow panel members at the recent ASA* Directors Forum. I have followed your work for several years and have recently completed a new script titled *Everything but the Groom*, which I believe meets your studio's standards for contemporary romantic comedy. (3) It is adapted from one of my own novels, which is currently available as an e-book through New Concepts Publishing.

(4) The premise of the story features Kate, a bridal consultant who is contracted to produce the wedding of the century at the private home of a wealthy family in Mill Valley, California. The catch? The too rich/too thin/too snooty bride is marrying Kate's former boyfriend and is taking every opportunity to flaunt her victory and push Kate's buttons. As if matters weren't difficult enough, Kate's regular photographer has an emergency that necessitates him sending an old army pal, Jack, to cover the nuptials. Jack, however, has his own agenda for being at the Murchie estate that day. (5)

(6) The time frame of the story covers 48 hours, there are no expensive special effects, and everything necessary for the wedding-day scene can easily be rented from—where else—any place in town that caters to real weddings.

(7) My publishing credits to date include 11 books, 97 plays and musicals, and more than 100 magazine and newspaper articles. I have also worked in radio and cable television, and I am currently teaching an online screen writing course through Fiction Writer's Connection (www.fictionwriters.com).
(8) Upon request, I would be happy to send you a treatment or the full script, along with a standard industry release.

I look forward to hearing from you at your earliest convenience.

Christina Hamlett

---

*ASA stands for American Screenwriters Association.

three agents have expressed interest in the project, which has been published as an e-book under the title *The Bridal Party*. The numbers within the text indicate important elements a query letter for a screenplay should have.

Analyzing the Query Letter

Following is an analysis of Christina's query letter.

1. Always address your query to a specific individual—and spell his or her name correctly.
2. It's always beneficial to mention a personal connection, whether to comment on a specific work, refer to a recent speech or article, or cite the name of someone who recommended that you initiate contact.
3. Film companies are always interested in bodies of work that have already been launched in another medium, so be sure to mention if this is the case.
4. Provide a brief overview of what your project is about.
5. Normally this query letter would contain one more sentence, explaining what Jack's agenda is. Agents and producers don't like teasers, but the author doesn't want to give away the surprise here.
6. Mention why the studio should take on this particular project. Remember that time, cost, and resources play a big part in what gets picked up and what gets dismissed.
7. Keep your background information brief, yet demonstrate that you've had enough experience for the studio to pay attention to you.
8. Never send a script unless asked. Many studios won't even open an envelope if it looks as if an unsolicited script might be enclosed.

THE ELEMENTS OF A SCREENPLAY

So far, we've talked about the tools you need to sell your screenplay, but what goes into a screenplay, what makes it salable, and what are producers looking for? Writer Elizabeth English provides some answers in excerpts from her article, "The Making of a Hollywood Film."

"What is the most important part of a screenplay?" asks Elizabeth. "According to [screenwriter] William Goldman, it's the first fifteen minutes, and/or the first fifteen pages—one page of a screenplay equals about one minute of film time. (Screenplays should snap, crackle, and pop on page one! Start with the story in motion, and that scene should foreshadow the story and the ending.) According to actor Paul Newman, though, the most important part of a movie is the last fifteen minutes. The message is clear—give your opening and conclusion equal attention, equal snap, crackle, and pop."

Screenplay Story Components

The article lists the six components of a screenplay, in order of importance.

1. Structure, a beginning, middle, and end (in three acts)
2. A bigger-than-life protagonist with whom the audience can identify
3. A well-defined conflict, introduced early on
4. A personal or life change experienced by the protagonist before the end of the first act
5. An antagonist(s) equal to or greater than the protagonist
6. The story's focus: start the story right before or in the middle of the most interesting part

Screenplay Story Structure

The article goes on to describe the story structure of your screenplay, act by act.

Act I should establish the protagonist and his or her story, setting up the protagonist's conflict or dilemma before introducing the other characters. The most conflict should be revealed at the end of the act, leaving the protagonist ready to move forward in a new direction.

The longest part of the screenplay is Act II, where the story really begins. This part of the screenplay is often difficult for writers. Elizabeth English writes, "Screenwriters sometimes have a lot of trouble with Act II. It can seem monotonous, episodic, or aimless. This may be because they've conceived of it as a series of obstacles to the hero's final goal, rather than as a dynamic series of events leading up to and trailing away from the central moment of death and rebirth. At the end of Act II, include the crisis at high point. Some realization of what's at stake has set in for the protagonist. There's a confrontation with the antagonist coming up. A moment of truth is about to occur."

She recommends that Act III should resolve all the conflicts in no more than fifteen minutes. "What's the hardest part of the script to write? The ending," she says. "The climax usually happens about one to five pages from the end of the script, followed by a short resolution that ties up all loose ends. The big finish, the problem is resolved, the question is answered, the tension lets up, and we know everything will be all right."

On the practical side, English advises following a standard Hollywood-required screenplay format. This includes using twelve-point Courier font on white, three-hole-punch paper, secured with two brass brads. The screenplay should be between ninety and one hundred twenty pages. Although the title is important, keep in mind that producers change titles very frequently.

What the Studios Look For

Elizabeth writes that most big studios look for formula movies aimed at their target audience of twelve- to twenty-four-year-old males. Executives try to put together package deals with major stars and/or an A-list director/producer.

Where Big-Studio Execs Get Their Material

The article lists the following sources of material for the big movie studios:

- Adaptations of bestsellers
- New versions of old films
- Sequels
- Copycat films
- TV spin-offs
- Comic books
- Foreign remakes

Original screenplays don't appear anywhere on the list. According to Elizabeth, the listed items are safer for studios based on audience recognition, and original work is a greater financial risk.

Film Festivals

Although film festivals might seem like little more than huge media events, they present opportunities for writers to try to sell their films or screenplays to distributors, buyers, producers, directors, investors, and actors. Screenwriters promote their work to the big studios, foreign markets, and production companies. It's a great chance to network and make new contacts.

Contacts

"Do you happen to know anyone in L.A.?" asks Elizabeth. "I mean even remotely connected to Hollywood film biz? A friend from school who is the gardener for the shrink of the waiter who serves lunch to the assistant of the guy who sweeps the floors at the office of the personal trainer for Richard Gere's hairdresser's boyfriend? Contacts mean everything."

Is There Hope?

Elizabeth English sums up by asking, "Here's the Big Question: What makes a film successful? Successful author and screenwriter William Goldman (*Butch Cassidy and the Sundance Kid*, *All the President's Men*) replies, (in an echoing, Godlike voice) the three words that ultimately define Hollywood: 'Nobody . . . knows . . . anything!'"

AN ALTERNATIVE TO THE BIG GUYS

Christina Hamlett, whose firsthand account appears later in this chapter, provides some valuable information to help you get your screenplay into the hands of interested people. To start with, she points out that major studios aren't the only option available to screenwriters.

If you are a serious film buff, you're well aware of independent films—there's even a television channel devoted to them. Christina explains, "By definition, an 'indie' is a filmmaker who raises his or her own money in order to finance and creatively control a chosen project. Driven by passion more than paycheck, many first-time directors and photographers cut their teeth on independent productions, savoring the heady joy of coloring outside of traditional lines to tell a story their own way.

"In contrast, the studio system assigns all creative decisions to executive producers and/or company heads who, in turn, dictate the style and policies for a hired director. Where studios have the luxury of big budgets, large crews, and Titanic-sized sets, indies function on $10,000 to $500,000 per picture, employ fewer than twenty technicians, and can comfortably fit into premises that would be daunted by gargantuan operations."

Although it's true that many major movie stars wouldn't accept a role in an indie, many are happy to earn a lower salary in exchange for the opportunity to explore a fascinating character and stretch their acting talent. Think of Forest Whitaker in *The Last King of Scotland*, or Nicole Kidman in *Dogville*—these are actors you might not expect to see working outside a big studio production, but they do.

According to Christina Hamlett, the growing number of indies around the country means that screenwriters can find an outlet close to home. Every state has a film commission, the original purpose of which is to assist in location shoots for studio productions. However, these commissions can also provide writers with information on local actors, investors, technical crew, and other writers. State film commissions benefit both the independent film company looking for regional talent and the screenwriter who is trying to promote a script or find work developing and revising new material.

"While there are obvious commercial advantages to tailoring projects to an indie's home turf, the only real limits are your imagination and the production's budget," Christina says.

"As an interesting side note, the book version of my screenplay, *Heaven Only Knows*, is set in San Francisco; the script was adapted to shift the story to the opposite coast. Not only was this beneficial in generating local excitement, but it also eliminated the exterior 'gotchas' of license plates, billboards, foliage, architecture, and weather (just some food for thought if you want to impress a director with your flexibility and sense of economy)."

Christina also mentions four additional options for finding potential directors for your script: trade magazines, screenwriting contests, film festivals, and online resources such as indiewire.com. The last two will give you the best opportunity for one-on-one interaction, as well as referrals to other filmmakers. Whichever route you choose, however, she advises that you remember this: "Cardinal rule: keep your sales pitch succinct. Nothing turns off a director faster than a rambling monologue that begins, 'Something happened to my father's aunt in Dubuque once that everyone says might make a funny movie.'"

Unlike studio productions, an agent isn't required to pitch a project to an indie. Screenwriters who write for indies generally have a much more active role in a film's development than would happen at a studio. Another difference is that indies don't only look for established material as a sure bet for a film. As Christina says, "Indies are in the business of pushing limits and thrusting lesser-known authors into the limelight, forever questing after that rough gem that will ignite into brilliance with just the right polish."

As her final advice, Christina sums up the "independent" spirit of indies. She says, "Although it's helpful to familiarize yourself with a director's past credits to gauge compatibility of your respective visions, it should in no way limit you from pitching your best work, no matter the genre or setting. Probably the worst mistake a writer can make is to assume that whatever genre of storytelling is currently selling will continue to sell. If a script is unique, it actually has a better chance of getting picked up than one that simply imitates ephemeral trends of aliens, talking babies, or Mother Nature run amok. To forget that indies march to their own distinct drummer can mean forfeiting the chance to see your title on a marquee."

DO YOU NEED AN AGENT?

You won't need an agent to pitch to the smaller, independent studios. But to target the big studios, you certainly will. You can find agents who handle screenplays listed in the *Guide to Literary Agents* (Writer's Digest Books) or the *Literary Marketplace*. If you already have an agent for a book project, check to see if he or she works with subagents for movie rights. Often an unpublished novel manuscript can be shown to film agents and producers and can capture interest—and perhaps a movie option—even if the book hasn't seen print.

Approach a new agent with a query letter (see the sample earlier in this chapter), and close it by offering to send your screenplay.

POTENTIAL EARNINGS

If Julia Roberts and Johnny Depp each earn $20 million per film, the writers working on their screenplays probably earn million-dollar salaries, too. But those writers have well-established reputations and have probably worked many times with studio executives who know their work.

An option on your novel (published or not) could earn you zero, $5,000, or $20,000. If the option is picked up, you could bank another $50,000 or $60,000, more if your project is actually made into a movie.

For an original screenplay, the 2006 *Writer's Market* survey reports that the average salary was $78,917, with a low of $54,854 and high of $102,980.

You can see from these figures that the overall money for writing screenplays isn't bad; it's just so hard to hit the mark that the chances of any money coming your way are pretty slim. But if you're tenacious and don't give up, the odds will be in your favor. Don't think in terms of one screenplay—or even twenty. The more prolific you are, the more you study the market and hone your craft, the more you know how to approach agents and producers, the bigger edge you give yourself.

FIRSTHAND ACCOUNT

Continue reading for more insight about the personal experience of a successful screenwriter.

CHRISTINA HAMLETT
Screenwriter

Christina Hamlett writes screenplays for Marcia & Company, an independent film studio in Maine. She has three screenplays currently under contract—*Changing Worlds*, *Muriel's Memoirs*, and *Where the Bodies Are*—as well as one musical, *The Last Princess*.

She has worked in all aspects of media, including cable television, radio scriptwriting, community news reporting, and advertising campaigns. She has also published twenty-one books, including *Could It Be a Movie?: How to Get Your Ideas from Out of Your Head and Up on the Screen*, and more than 100 magazine and newspaper articles. She has written 112 plays and musicals. She does a humor column for several national and regional publications and has worked as an actress and theater director.

She received her B.A. in communications, specializing in audience analysis and message design, from California State University, Sacramento.

Getting Started

Christina has always loved a good story, whether it's been a book that has kept her reading until three in the morning or a movie that surprised and delighted her with the quality of its writing and plot twists. She began writing play scripts in the late 1970s for her touring theater company, The Hamlett Players. This gave her the opportunity to test material on audiences and also to see what sort of interpretation the actors would apply to their lines and characters. In this way she could tell whether what sounded perfect in her own head might sound very different from what she intended when spoken by an actor.

She says, "I'm drawn to film because of my affinity for visuals and dynamic dialogue, not to mention that one day I'm determined to write a part that only Mel Gibson or Tom Selleck can play (and which will require substantive one-on-one coaching by the author). The common—and yet intoxicating—denominator of all movies, of course, is that none of them would exist without a screenwriter sitting down to a keyboard somewhere and typing, 'EXTERIOR, TWILIGHT, THE CASTLE . . .'"

Christina's first job after high school was writing movie and play reviews for a weekly newspaper in Northern California. It not only gave her a byline (and free tickets) and provided a worthwhile overview of both good and bad productions, but it also whet her appetite to see her own name on the big screen. She got the job by convincing the editor that she could provide a fresh voice on the performing arts. This job led to a long stint in community theater, the management of her own acting company, and then on to screenwriting.

Answering an inquiry posted on the Internet led to her working with an independent company. An ambitious young filmmaker on the Eastern Seaboard wanted to hear from anyone who had written scripts in the genres of comedy or romance. She says, "My initial impression was that this person was an acne-faced teenage boy with a camcorder shooting dinosaur-model videos in his parents' garage. I replied to the post just to be encouraging and to offer advice. I was definitely wrong—about the gender, the age, the credentials, and the extent of the dream."

Christina and the filmmaker began an e-mail correspondence that led to her pitching the synopsis of an unpublished manuscript, one that editors at every major house had rejected with the excuse, 'What we're really looking for are books that can be adapted to film.' Less than two months after that first exchange of notes, *Heaven Only Knows* was a screenplay in preproduction and Christina was lead screenwriter for Marcia & Company.

The Realities of the Work

"It's a glorious feeling to get paid for doing work you really love," says Christina. "In fact, if it's a perfect fit, it doesn't seem like work at all!"

She believes that working with an indie producer provided much more feedback and creative control than she'd find at a major studio. She and the producer, who live on separate coasts, brainstorm by e-mail. They share a common vision of what quality family entertainment should be. Christina has introduced a talented composer in New Mexico to write original songs and scores for the team. She feels that what clicks in this trio of professional dynamics is that, at any given time, two of the partners are thinking that the third person is really the one with all the talent.

Christina's primary area of expertise is comedy, which she describes as portraying regular, workaday people caught up in ludicrous situations made all the worse by their attempts to pretend that they have everything under perfect control. She admits that her plots and characters are derived from years of people-watching and speculating "What if?" She says, "My own life has been replete with enough odd relatives, neighbors, and coworkers to keep me supplied with funny lines and scenarios for decades. They, of course, never recognize themselves in print nor on screen. I'm also fortunate to have a husband who enjoys critiquing my projects and assisting me when I've written myself into mental cul-de-sacs."

Christina says that her primary job is to come up with commercial ideas that will work as films. Every project begins with a rough outline, a lot of give-and-take brainstorming, discussion of potential actors and shooting locales, and then the development of an actual 120-page screenplay.

Although she has an open invitation to visit the set whenever she wants, Christina has enough confidence in the producer's talent and judgment to not have to be physically present when those cameras start rolling. In turn, the producer has the assurance of Christina's flexibility that if a scene isn't working, she'll have a faxed or e-mailed revision in her hands by the time the crew gets back from break. She finds that there's actually an advantage to being geographically separated from the production, since the distance keeps her from becoming too involved with the day-to-day minutiae of the set.

She says that there's no such thing as a typical or boring day in the film business and insists that it's the most fun thing she's ever done. When she's at home, Christina is usually working on her next script idea or on any number of freelance projects, including magazine articles and books. When she's on a set, she is generally absorbed with watching how the elements come together, as well as watching dailies and offering input on which scenes work and which don't.

The Upsides and Downsides

Christina's take on the ups and downs of her work are best stated in her own words. As she says, "Besides the aforementioned joy of seeing a story I've written leap off the printed page and spring to life with real actors, props, and sets, I also subscribe to the philosophy that success is the best revenge. What sweet knowledge it is to picture the reaction of ex-boyfriends, crabby ex-bosses, and snooping former office mates whenever my name scrolls up a screen in capital letters.

"I also view this job as an opportunity to one day segue back into acting by subtly writing into every script a role for a stunning, slender, older woman with quick wit and big hair. What I enjoy least is that there aren't enough hours in the day to write everything that I want!"

Earnings

Christina explains that working for an independent film company, her salary is negotiable and contingent on the total operating budget of the movie. It includes a percentage of the budget plus a percentage of profits. In a case where the company has bought only the screenplay rights, she retains the freedom to negotiate book, theater, and additional subsidiary rights on her own.

Advice from a Professional

Christina strongly advises knowing the craft and format inside and out before you ever send out a query letter to an independent producer. She stresses that just because indies are often viewed as stepping stones does not mean that the quality of the work submitted can be inferior.

She also suggests that you write constantly and see as many films as you can. Read scripts whenever possible. Put your best energy into writing the kind of story you yourself would pay those high box-office prices to see.

Don't go into screenwriting with the sole objective of making a lot of money, Christina warns. Go into it with the spirit that you want to have fun doing something you really enjoy, and you'll definitely be rewarded.

"Most of all," she says, "never forget that the script is the backbone, the essence, the very reason that cameras roll, directors direct, stars are born, and magic unfolds every night on the screens of theaters across the country. Without the writer, audiences would be left sitting in the dark."

THREE HELPFUL TIPS

Based on all the advice you've read from professional screenwriters, keep these three tips in mind as you plan your career:

• Learn as much as you can. Read screenplays and books on how to write them, and take a screenwriting course.

• Be sure your query letter is professional and includes all the pertinent information about your screenplay.

• Remember that independent studios and production companies are often receptive to the work of new screenwriters.

TECHNICAL WRITING

"The difference between the right word and the almost right word is the
difference between lightning and the lightning bug."

–Mark Twain

Technical writing may be considered one of our oldest forms of communication. Early technical communicators used cave drawings to convey information about such things as how their tools worked and what they were used for.

Modern technology has become much more complex, and it's rare for a single picture to be worth the proverbial thousand words. Today's technical writers are faced with the task of making scientific and technical information easily understandable to a nontechnical audience. They prepare operating and maintenance manuals, catalogs, parts lists, assembly instructions, sales-promotion materials, and project proposals. They also plan and edit technical reports and oversee preparation of illustrations, photographs, diagrams, and charts.

To many people, however, "good technical writing" is an oxymoron. Mirroring the Mark Twain quote at the beginning of this chapter, the difference between good technical writing and not so good can have global impact, as you will see in "Good Technical Writing Should Not Be an Oxymoron," an article contributed for this book by writer and engineer Lisa Eagleson-Roever.

GOOD TECHNICAL WRITING SHOULD NOT BE AN OXYMORON

"Despite the numerous comic strips Scott Adams, creator of Dilbert, has used to poke fun at it, technical writing is not limited to jargon-filled reports translatable only by engineers and nuclear scientists," Lisa writes. "Technical writing includes any form of business communication not intended to be advertising. Reports, letters, internal memos, guidelines, procedures, training material, and manuals are part of the technical-writing genre.

"Good technical writing, even at its most technical, should not be written to confuse the reader. The letter in Figure 7.1 is a typical business

Figure 7.1: Technical Writing Sample

Babcock & Wilcox Company

IR Generation Group

TO: [name—Manager, Plant Integration, Three Mile Island]

FROM: [name—Manager, Plant Performance Services, Babcock & Wilcox]

Subject: Operator Interruption of High Pressure Injection (HPI)

References: [two titles listed]

References 1 and 2 recommend a change in Babcock & Wilcox's philosophy for HPI system use during low-pressure transits. Basically they recommend leaving the HPI pumps on, once HPI has been indicated, until it can be determined that the hot leg temperature is more than 50°F below Tsat for the reactor cooling system (RCS) pressure. Nuclear Service believes that this mode can cause the RCS (including the pressurizer) to be solid. The pressure reliefs will lift, with a water surge through the discharge piping into the quench tank.

We believe the following incidents should be evaluated:

1. If the pressurizer goes solid with one or more HPI pumps continuing to operate, would there be a pressure spike before the relief valves open that could cause damage to the RCS?

2. What damage would the water surge through the relief valve discharge piping and quench tank cause?

To date, the Nuclear Service has not notified our operating plants to change HPI policy consistent with References 1 and 2 because of the above-stated questions. Yet the references suggest the possibility of uncovering the core if present HPI policy is continued. We request that Integration resolve the issue of how the HPI system should be used. We are available to help as needed.

[signed]

letter, but one that proved to be dangerously ineffective. This letter is part of public record:

"Did you actually read all that? Probably not. Neither did the plant manager at Three Mile Island.

"That letter was Babcock & Wilcox Company's way of warning Three Mile Island that they could uncover the reactor's core (and thus possibly have a nuclear meltdown) if certain operating procedures were not changed. As you may remember, a nuclear meltdown is exactly what happened."

How to Make Your Writing "Good" Technical Writing

Lisa recommends using clear, standard language and simple sentences. Define all acronyms and special or technical terms, and avoid the use of any work-related jargon or slang. Related items should be put in a list, rather then in a long paragraph, and graphs are best for displaying complex information. In the example above, the writer did define acronyms but didn't use clear language and simple sentences.

You Have Ten Seconds to Make a Point

Since the average reader takes only ten seconds to scan a document for its purpose before deciding what to do with it, the purpose should be stated up front, either as an opening sentence or on the "Re:" line.

"BWC failed miserably at being up front," Lisa says. "In court, a recipient of the above memo stated that he didn't remember receiving it. Even when it was shown to him and he was told that there was proof he had received it, he still didn't remember ever having read it.

"But, looking at the memo, it's sadly understandable. The point of BWC's memo is in the third-to-last sentence in the last paragraph. The 'Re:' line does not list the key message. If instead it had read 'Possibility of Uncovering Core Exists' the Plant Manager might have paid attention. He understood what could happen if the core were uncovered."

Given this ten-second rule, you should consider how your document looks on the page. Keep sentences to no more than twenty words and paragraphs to about six lines. Write in active voice, which sounds better to the reader and makes the document easier to read. Topics should be highlighted by headings, which make the document easier to scan.

When You Want Action from the Reader

"If you want action from your reader, make certain your purpose contains the phrase 'request for,'" writes Lisa. "Put it at the beginning of your document and again at the end. Often managers and executives skip over the middle of a document and scan only the first and last paragraphs. If they do not see key words like 'request' they will likely put it aside for later. And that means they may never read it again.

"Note that BWC's request is at the bottom of the memo, in the second-to-last sentence. If it had been under a header or on a line by itself, the plant manager at Three Mile Island might have seen it when he scanned the document."

Know Who's Reading Your Documents

Lisa points out that many writers neglect to think of who beyond the initial recipient will read their document. She says, "With the increasing ease of attaching documents to e-mail, it's likely your report could land on five continents in three days. If your company has offices, manufacturing sites, or distribution centers in other countries, you should assume that your document will leave the United States."

This makes the use of standard language in technical writing even more important. Consider how what you write might be understood by someone with only a minimal understanding of English.

In summary, Lisa writes, "And even when your international business partners speak English as a first language or speak fluent English as a second language, read your document carefully before sending it off. American English and British English, for example, use many of the same words for different purposes—some of which are in no way related to each other. Note too that Europeans and Indians who learn English at a young age are more likely to understand Britishisms and Canadianisms than Americanisms."

MAKING A NAME FOR YOURSELF

Will you become famous as a technical writer? It's highly unlikely. In fact, technical writers are often, by necessity, anonymous authors who do not get to see their byline attached to their work. (The exceptions are people who write scientific or technical articles for newspapers, magazines, and scholarly publications under their own names or write popular how-to guides.)

Why are technical writers unacknowledged? The next time you try to assemble a child's toy or a new barbecue grill, try to program your DVD player or hook up your new fax machine, look on the instruction booklet for the name of the person responsible for the directions—the person you'd like to contact to complain. You won't find it. But that aside, the goal of most employers who produce technical material is to reach their audience with concise and easy-to-understand language, to promote their product, or to train their audience in its use. No writing stars are required or encouraged.

You can build a name for yourself, though, through your list of credits. Every assignment you land and complete becomes another line to add to your résumé. In some cases you might even be able to keep a sample of your work and create a professional portfolio to show to new clients. Word of mouth and employer and client references and recommendations will also help you to become known in your area of specialization.

JOB TITLES

Although the term *technical writer* is the most common job title used, there are other titles as well as ranks:

Assistant Technical Writer	Information Systems Writer
Associate Technical Writer	Instructional Designer
Consulting Technical Writer	Junior Technical Writer
Copyeditor	Knowledge Analyst
Copywriter	Lead Technical Writer
Corporate Technical Writer	Senior Technical Writer
Course Developer	Software Technical Writer
Curriculum Designer	Technical Communicator
Curriculum Planner	Technical Editor
Documentation Contractor	Technical Intern
Documentation Specialist	Technical Translator
Education Specialist	Trainer

TECHNICAL WRITING FIELDS

The number of areas in which a technical writer can work are vast and varied. Most technical writers specialize in just one, or sometimes two, areas.

A software manual writer wouldn't be expected to be knowledgeable about the environment or advertising, just as a medical writer wouldn't necessarily be familiar with auto mechanics.

The following list of fields is just a guide. Your own research will no doubt help you add to the list.

Advertising	Journalism
Agriculture	Manual Writing
Architecture	Manufacturing
Armed Forces	Market Research
Corporate Communications	Mechanics
Computer System	Medicine
Documentation	Multimedia Specialist
Education	Pharmaceuticals
Electronics	Proposal Writing
Engineering	Publication Management and
Entertainment	Design
Environment	Publicity
Film and Documentaries	Public Relations
Finance and Banking	Research Firms
Graphic Design	Sales
Government	Science
Information Developer	Telecommunications
Instructional Design	Video Production
Insurance	Web Page Authoring and Site
Investments	Design

Job Locations

Many technical writers work for computer software firms or manufacturers of aircraft, chemicals, pharmaceuticals, and computers and other electronic equipment. Technical writers are employed throughout the country, but the largest concentrations are in the Northeast, Texas, and California.

TECHNICAL EDITORS

Most companies differentiate between technical writing and technical editing. Editing requires a person who is adept at improving the composition of writing—correcting grammar, punctuation, style, and construction of sentences and paragraphs. Technical writing, on the other hand, encompasses the whole process. It takes in editing, of course, but it extends to original writing as well as the rewriting of other people's manuscripts. The writer must have a firm grasp of the technical material to cope with this kind of assignment.

For the somewhat restricted job of technical editing, a solid background in English composition will serve you well. Of course, to succeed in this field you should also possess an affinity for technological subjects and familiarity with engineering and scientific terms. A firm foundation in science and engineering is essential if you will deal in depth with technical subjects.

Many technical writers work with engineers on technical subject matter to prepare written interpretations of engineering and design specifications and other information for a general readership. They may also serve as part of a team conducting usability studies to help improve the design of a product that is in the prototype stage. They also plan and edit technical materials and oversee the preparation of illustrations, photographs, diagrams, and charts.

CAREER OUTLOOK

Opportunities are expected to be very good for technical writers and those with training in a specialized field through 2014. Demand for technical writers is expected to increase because of the continuing expansion of scientific and technical information and the need to communicate it to others. Legal, scientific, and technological developments and discoveries generate demand for people to interpret technical information for a more general audience.

Rapid growth and change in the high-technology and electronics industries result in a greater need for people to write user's guides, instruction manuals, and training materials. This work requires people who not only are technically skilled as writers, but also are familiar with the subject area.

TRAINING

Increasingly, technical writing requires a degree in, or some knowledge about, a specialized field, such as engineering, business, or one of the sciences. In many cases, people with good writing skills can acquire - specialized knowledge on the job. Some transfer from jobs as technicians, scientists, or engineers, while others begin as research assistants or trainees in a technical information department, develop technical communication skills, and then assume writing duties.

COURSES IN TECHNICAL WRITING

Depending on the university, you will find courses in technical writing offered in many different departments, including English, other humanities-based departments, communications, journalism, business, the sciences, and engineering.

Over the years, colleges and other schools have recognized that students majoring in technical subjects such as engineering, for example, should be taught courses in technical writing in addition to their regular courses in English composition. Technical writing courses are usually taught by members of the English department in an engineering college or by teachers of engineering who have an interest in writing. They deal with special forms of technical writing such as report writing and the preparation of scientific papers and magazine articles.

As a result of the formation of various technical writing societies and the great need for technical writers, industry and technical presses have taken more interest in what is being taught in colleges. Every year the Institute of Electrical and Electronics Engineers (IEEE), a global organization with more than 350,000 members, holds a special session titled "Engineering Writing and Speech." During this session, seminars and panel discussions on the training of engineers are held to foster clearer and more informative written communications and to improve the relationships between engineers and technical writers. The result of this two-way process has been the introduction of many fine technical writing courses and four-year programs into a number of colleges and universities.

In addition to technical writing courses, a growing number of schools now offer majors in this specific discipline. The programs have been given various names and can be found in communication- or humanities-oriented departments under such course titles as science writing, science information, technical journalism, and technical communications.

The salaries offered to students seeking first jobs in technical writing cannot be definitely established; however, certain basic principles do apply:

• A student with a bachelor's or master's degree in engineering or science can command a higher beginning salary than a student with a degree in English or some other nontechnical subject.

• Graduates from certain prestigious colleges usually can command higher salaries than students from lesser-known schools.

• Higher salaries will go to students who have the highest grade point averages, who have more summer work experience, and who can display the characteristics of ability and initiative.

• Technical writers with degrees in certain areas, notably electrical engineering and electronics, are in greater demand than those with training in other areas.

• Beginning technical writers are likely to be evaluated very closely on the basis of their educational records, their writing ability, and their potential for being promoted.

According to the Society for Technical Communication (STC), the median annual salary for entry-level technical writers was $42,500 in 2004. The median annual salary for midlevel nonsupervisory technical writers was $51,500, and for senior nonsupervisory technical writers, $66,000. The same source reports that technical writers in Canada had average annual earnings of $58,190 in 2003.

Median earnings for salaried technical writers were $53,490 in 2004, with most earning between $41,440 and $68,980.

For freelancers, the 2006 *Writers Market* survey reports average hourly earnings of $53; the low salary reported was $25 an hour, and the high was $75 an hour.

Freelance medical and science writers reported average hourly earnings of $78, with a low of $30 and high of $125. On a per-project basis, this group had average earnings of $2,520; the low salary was $800 and the high was $4,800.

The average salary for a three-chapter engineering manual was $23,500.

THE JOB HUNT

It's a very good idea to consider employment opportunities long before you graduate from college. If you are seriously thinking about becoming a technical writer, you can take a number of steps that will help you obtain professional guidance and information:

• Contact the Education Committee of the Society for Technical Communication. The committee exists to inform people how to prepare themselves for the profession; it is ready to answer your questions and will provide the names of prominent members of the society to whom you may write for advice. The STC also maintains a job bank. Their contact information is provided in Appendix A.

• The STC provides various publications on many different aspects of technical writing.

• If you are in high school, make an appointment with your guidance counselor to discuss the profession of technical writing. A lot depends on whether you are planning to continue your education by going to college or taking other specialized training courses. In either case, counselors should have literature available about technical writing careers or can tell you where to find it.

• Don't be shy about talking to professional technical writers or professors of technical writing. This type of information gathering will help you to be sure you're on the right track with your career choice.

• If you are in college, visit the job placement office. Throughout the year, college placement offices are in contact with the human resources managers of companies and other organizations that are looking for people to fill important technical writing jobs.

• Establish job contacts by getting in direct touch with the supervisors and administrators of the publications departments of companies that employ technical writers. To establish these contacts, read the large industrial ads for technical writers in newspapers or online, especially those in highly developed industrial areas. If you can't find a specific name to send your inquiry to, send it to the director of publications. In time, your letter will filter through to the right person, and you will be able to set up an informational interview—which could possibly lead to a job contract or a full-time job.

• Search the Internet for job opportunities. Websites and databases are updated on a regular basis. The following are websites of agencies and organizations that will help make your job search a bit easier.

The Computer Merchant Ltd.
tcml.com

Documentation Strategies, Inc.
docstrats.com

Essential Data Corp.
essentialdata.com

PVA Global
pvaglobal.com

Sample Job Advertisements

To give you an idea of the types of jobs that are advertised, the following samples have been culled from various website databases. Identifying information has been omitted because the jobs will now be filled.

Position: Technical Writer

Location: Maryland

Job Type: Full-time

Salary: Depends on experience

Description: Experienced Technical Writer who can support several projects IT documentation needs for this BI/DW program hosting health-care-centric data and metrics. Develop technical documentation for the project; identify and create documentation templates for use by the team; review/edit all written documentation and deliverables; assist Quality Assurance Manager with project audits.

Requirements: Excellent written and verbal communication skills; three-plus years of technical writing experience; strong knowledge of Microsoft Word, PowerPoint, Visio, and Adobe Acrobat; ability to learn new applications/software quickly for purposes of documentation; ability to read programming languages such as Java and Oracle

PL/SQL; ability to multitask; ability to work individually and as part of a team; bachelor's degree in English, Computer Science, or related field required.

Position: Technical Writer/Business Analyst

Location: Texas

Job Type: Contract

Description: Document current systems by using technical code to write documentation about what the programs do and how they work together in the system. Documentation will be written in MS Word. A major part of the documentation will need to be completed by mid-February, 2007, but updates will be needed through March 2007. Contract extension may be possible.

Requirements: Technical writing expertise in a Web environment, proficiency in writing (SQL code, Stored Procedures, and DTS packages), ability to analyze and document (workflows, processes, and procedures), ability to complete disaster recovery plans, excellent communication skills and interaction with others, understanding of code (written in Java, ASP, C/C++, Cold Fusion, ActiveX, VB, HTML/DHTML), understanding of applications (COM/DCOM, CORBA, and linking back-end applications); technical coding background in the above is a plus.

Position: Technical Writer

Location: Massachusetts

Job Type: Part-time, permanent

Salary: $35,000–$45,000

Description: This position is twenty hours per week with full health/dental and life insurance benefits. We are seeking a Technical Writer to create all printed and online technical documentation for end users including user guides, quick-start guides, release notes, readme docs, help guides, technical briefs, and the occasional white paper. You will identify, plan for, and revise technical writing project requirements and research complex source material for these projects. You will also be responsible for coordinating the display of graphics and the production and translations of documents. If you are qualified and interested in this position, please apply online today for immediate consideration.

Requirements: Candidates must have proven skills in creating complex technical documents, project management experience and skills, a BA/BS degree, and four or more years of Help development experience to include online help, release notes, software installation guides, user guides, reference guides, administrator guides, and quick-reference materials. You must possess fundamental knowledge of the business processes, systems, and philosophy associated with high-performance, high-technology companies.

Position: Proposal Writer/Technical Writer

Location: Georgia

Job Type: Contract

Salary: $24.00 per hour

Description: Create, maintain, and update standard proposal templates for service lines and all business partners with minor changes to templates and services. Write nonstandard proposals utilizing sections of templates to build a nonstandard proposal. Utilize Operations or Sales Executives for objectives and deliverables for proposal content. Proofread and quality check all proposals. Interact with legal counsel to resolve issues surrounding preparation of proposals. Interact with business partners to finalize proposals. Work with internal executives on preparation of proposals. Respond to RFPs using standard proposal content and previous RFP responses. Coordinate with Sales/Operations on content.

Requirements: Previous proposal writing experience; health-care background preferred. Experience with large consulting contracts and/or paralegal; excellent verbal and written communication skills; ability to multitask and meet deadlines in a timely manner.

Position: Technical Writer/Editor

Location: Connecticut

Job Type: Full-time

Description: The right candidate will provide experienced technical writing/editing support to federal client for RDT&E documents, reports, etc. Ability to take complex subjects and make them readable for a wide variety of audiences.

Requirements: Bachelor's degree in technical writing or related field; minimum of six years' experience. Excellent computer skills and experience using MS Office Suite required. Analysis of data and ability to work in diverse formats. Must have excellent communication skills, strong attention to detail, and ability to work closely with others in a demanding team environment. Some experience in developing PR and Marketing materials/documentation helpful. Experience working with the government or state desired.

Position: Technical Writer

Location: Virginia

Job Type: Full-time

Description: As a technical writer with the Training and Documentation team, you will ensure the accuracy, consistency, and overall excellence of the layout, writing, and production of our internal technical documents such as operating, maintenance, and reaction procedures. Under supervision, you will rework drafts or create appropriate original copy consistent with professional, effective technical writing using various information-gathering methods including interviews, observations, and independent research. You will also develop methods for writing and editing documents appropriate to a specific training purpose, audience, and delivery method. You will develop project management techniques for organizing and managing complex, ongoing projects, including managing priorities on a daily basis; collaborating with subject matter experts, engineers, and technicians; identifying and coordinating review loops; validating information; and ensuring timely project completion.

Requirements: To be successful in this position, you must exhibit a strong command of the English language and the proper use of grammar, punctuation, and spelling; familiarity with standard proofreaders' marks; and beginner-level knowledge of Adobe FrameMaker and other software and applications routinely used in the creation of technical documentation such as Acrobat, Illustrator, Office, HTML, and other products as needed. Education: Bachelor's degree in

English, Communication, Technical Communication, Writing, Journalism, or a related writing field†or a minimum of three years of strong writing background relating to the specific job functions. Please provide three writing samples along with your application.

Contract Versus Full-Time

As you can see from the sample job advertisements, many employers are looking for short-term help, usually from three to six months. Technical writers who accept these positions are, in essence, freelancers. They contract themselves out to a variety of companies; when one job is finished, they go on to the next. Some people prefer contracting and find it a very agreeable way to make a living. It often pays better, although benefits are seldom included, and offers a variety of assignments and experience in different areas.

Other people get into contracting as a foot in the door to a new job market and make the move to permanent employment as quickly as they can. Some technical writers choose contracting because their company downsized and left them unemployed. Some hope to take something permanent as soon as it's offered.

From the employers' standpoint, contracting can be more cost-effective than keeping full-time technical writers on staff. If they subcontract with other companies to produce specific, time-limited projects, it makes sense for them to budget the fee for a freelancer into their proposal. And with any part-time employment contract, they often can save themselves the cost of health insurance, sick days, pension plans, and other perks offered to full-time help.

Telecommuting

Technical writers who prefer to work at home can find employment where telecommuting is allowed. Telecommuting can mean anything from working almost entirely at home via an ISDN line to your company, meaning that you have a direct connection to their network, to being able to take work home with you occasionally. You must, of course, have your own computer with the appropriate applications. If you don't have any meetings scheduled and you have enough input to proceed, you can work at home, writing without interruption for a day or more.

FIRSTHAND ACCOUNTS

Read what these professional technical writers have to say about their careers—maybe something will strike a chord with you.

BARBARA KARST-SABIN
Senior Technical Writer

Barbara Karst-Sabin works on a contract basis for a variety of high-tech companies, focusing mainly on writing online documentation for Web-based businesses. She worked for the government for several years, first as a technical writer in telecommunications, then in various other technologies. She has also worked as a medical writer. With most of her contracts she is able to telecommute one or two days a week. She has been writing since the late 1970s and earned her master's degree in technical writing and editing in 1986 from San Francisco State University.

Getting Started

After a brief career as an artist, Barbara got a job at a medical school. With her background in biochemistry and general science, she found work in the editorial office of the Department of Neurosurgery. Because her bachelor's degree in art kept her from being hired as a medical writer, Barbara decided to enroll in graduate school.

At that time, the only master's program in technical/science writing was offered at Penn State, but she found a program to suit her needs at San Francisco State University. To qualify, applicants had to develop a set of courses that would provide the required background, but the courses had to come from more than one school. In addition, three people in the field had to review the proposed curriculum and agree that it would suffice and that the applicant would be able to do the job once the program was completed. Barbara met all the requirements and found herself with one of the few master's degrees in technical writing and editing.

By the time she finished her graduate program, Barbara had passed a test for a government job and was offered a position as a tech writer in telecommunications back East. She accepted the job and hasn't done any more medical writing.

Getting a Job

Barbara returned to California after working in Arizona for a while. Without any contacts or experience in that area, she started working on contracts. She found her first one while working a contract as a training coordinator in the same company. Now she contacts a recruiter she likes working with and posts a notice of availability on the Internet so that headhunters can contact her.

She has gotten jobs through referrals by friends and even found one with a company where she interviewed for a permanent position before it downsized and released most of its writers. When the company was looking for contractors, the manager remembered Barbara and offered her a contract job.

The Realities of the Work

Barbara says that technical writing is ideal for her because she loves to write and loves learning how things work. Barbara has written programmer's guides for telecommunications switches, end-user guides for software, troubleshooting manuals for military field communications equipment, recommendations to the Executive Branch on where to spend their science research money in five years, and a review of some of the diagnostic tools used in severe head injuries. In addition, she developed training courses in the counter-narcotics field and in gourmet and specialty foods. She has also created a website on a company's intranet for their internal documentation and has written and produced video news and documentaries.

She has been assigned to several projects for which she was on loan to complete a specific job. In most jobs, however, she is the lead writer. Barbara has also worked on several jobs as sole writer, which are usually with a group or company that has never had a writer on staff and doesn't have much documentation. In these situations, she assesses the problem and determines the best strategy to accomplish the task in a limited amount of time.

Barbara points out that most tech writers have to attend regular product and department meetings but spend more of their time in their cubicles. Sometimes they spend time in the labs learning more about equipment or software, and they must definitely spend time working with engineers to get the information they need to write their pieces.

The more usual tech writing jobs involve following a style guide and previous documentation to produce a finite number of document types, each of which has certain required types of information to be presented in dictated ways: for example, step-by-step instructions for installing software and reconfiguring a system.

In most cases, publications managers spend a lot of time in meetings, planning their department's work and allocating resources. Many of them do no writing at all and may not even be writers. In the high-tech sector, though, the writer is generally part of the entire product-development process, attending meetings from the time a product is first planned. Writers negotiate their deadlines based on the deliverables set by the engineering and marketing members and may work with the engineers during development to begin roughing out their books.

Many writers act as usability testers, and may be the first to see problems or faults and can call them to the developer's attention. They frequently get the product even before the Quality Assurance (QA) people do. On the other hand, the QA staff can help review the writers' documents for accuracy, since they are as deeply involved in the internal workings of the product (hardware or software) as the developers. Because of this working relationship, QA and Tech Publications are often paired under the same management.

The Upsides and Downsides

Barbara enjoys the variety that contracting offers, feeling that she would be bored by a permanent job where she'd spend all her time writing and updating the same kind of manuals. A big company that offers opportunities to move within the organization can help fend off the trap of sameness. She says that although many people feel comfortable working within a routine, "I'm really good at the jobs where they hand you a whip and a chair and throw you in with the lions. It's what I built my reputation on in my government job and the reason I got to do so many different things.

"I'm good at big-picture thinking and at processes—that is, I can usually tell pretty quickly where the process has broken down, and I'm organized enough to know how to fix it. This isn't for everyone, and that's a good thing—more work for me!"

Barbara feels that bad management is one of the main downsides of the job. Corporate philosophy often seems to be that tech writers can't be managers, so the company assigns a former production person who may be good at meeting deadlines and getting a book ready to be published but whose linear thinking precludes seeing the best way to present the material. This can cause documents to suffer, and the writer is the one who takes the hit.

The technical writing process is frequently a chaotic one. Barbara once spent four months at a very high salary trying to prepare a document that never came to be. It took her three months to get the engineers to admit that they couldn't make the product work and weren't sure what it would look like or exactly what it would do when it was finished. Despite this, management still blamed Barbara for wasting their money. In her opinion, too many managers seem to forget that the writer doesn't work in a vacuum.

Earnings

Barbara works in the Silicon Valley, where salaries in technical writing are higher than anywhere else. As a senior writer, she has earned $65 per hour; a junior writer would most likely start at about $35 an hour. Writers who work independently and don't have an agency fee included in their rate can make much more.

Barbara advises that when you translate contract dollars into actual salary, you should expect to drop about one-third of the total amount. For example, if you earn $60 per hour (approximately $125,000 a year) doing contract work, you would ask prospective full-time employers for an annual salary of $80,000.

She also acknowledges that she has been fortunate to climb up the salary ladder quickly—within one year of her first job she'd gone from $40 to $60 an hour, based on her extensive background.

Barbara says, "Part of the secret, even for a good, experienced writer, is not being afraid to ask for what you're worth. Also, contracting, because of the frequent moves, is probably the best way to move up the 'billable' ladder."

Advice from a Professional

Barbara stresses that a successful technical writer needs to be able to express complex ideas in simple terms. You must have an interest in technology and be able to pick up new concepts quickly. You have to be willing to work hard—to learn, to deal with people, to meet deadlines.

She recommends taking a certificate program that will give you exposure to the main kinds of applications commonly used and to the standard document formats—documentation plan, installation guide, user's/administrator's/programmer's guide. This is enough to get you in the door.

Students in certificate programs can get technical writing internships to help them get professional experience. Other than that, even those with a great deal of technical background might have to start at the bottom. However, once they have proven themselves as technical writers, they can quickly move up to an intermediate or even senior position, but they'll probably have to change jobs to do it.

Barbara also recommends joining the STC, which offers regularly updated job listings. She sees newspaper want ads as a last resort, since online methods are the most cost-effective in terms of your time and energy. When you go that way, a lot of companies will do a screening interview by phone first, saving you a lot of running around. Network if you know other writers or people in the industry you're targeting.

JIM COCHRAN
Technical Writer/Producer/Director

Jim Cochran owns his own company, Communications Arts, in Albuquerque, New Mexico. Most of the writing he does is for electronic media, such as video or CD-ROM, with the occasional print article. He deals with a wide variety of scientific, medical, and technical materials. He has been working in the field since 1979.

Getting Started

Jim's first project was to help the U.S. Department of Agriculture explain Title IX, one of their small-farmer grant programs. He followed this by writing ad copy and developing scripts for marketing and training videos. He enjoyed the visual and creative aspects of production and found that he had a talent for understanding complex technical processes, breaking them down into steps, and describing them to defined audiences.

The Realities of the Work

The common aspect among Jim's jobs is learning about a process and describing it to a specific audience. He uses a wide variety of writing styles and presentation techniques within the genre. He writes articles for magazines, copy for marketing materials, both print and electronic, and scripts for CD-ROM and video.

Working as an independent producer, he moves from project to project, preferring those that involve developing descriptive presentations. Along the way, Jim has developed expertise in nuclear-waste disposal, visual representation of computer processes, and training or orienting people to newly developed programs such as training actuaries on how to explain 401(k) offerings or an overview video for the Defense Department on their new computerized travel system.

During his first meeting with a client, Jim asks some pointed questions and helps to focus the client on the answers. He tries to understand what the client wishes to communicate, to whom, and why. He feels that one of the most important steps in this process is making clients see that you understand what they've told you, even if it means repeating it verbatim, in order to establish trust.

The next step is to develop a presentation concept that he likes, including as much as possible, such as stories, animations, celebrity spokespersons, exotic locations, and so forth. "Then sell it," Jim says. "There is nothing more important nor seductive than vision. It doesn't matter if the idea you started out with requires Mel Gibson as your spokesman in Hawaii, and it ends up with a narrator and shots of the factory floor. The clients will appreciate that they have a visionary working for them. Of course, only experience will give you the ability to know how much the big things cost, but throw them out there. Sell only ideas you're in love with. It will make your work a joy."

The Upsides and Downsides

Jim enjoys the process of gathering information, the collaborative development of the visual presentation, and the high-profile nature of the end product.

He also appreciates the opportunity to work with other people who are good at what they do. Although technicians and engineers are often perceived as dry, Jim takes it as a personal challenge to discover where their excitement for their expertise lies. He believes that there is a point when people describing a complex process light up and begin to talk faster as they visualize something complex, yet beautiful in its simplicity. It's what they are visualizing that Jim wants to capture, because that's what will communicate to the audience.

Jim dislikes when clients tell him they don't want a presentation to be too flashy, and they underestimate the intelligence of their audience. He doesn't enjoy it when he can't get the cooperation from content sources, or when the client changes his or her mind about the nature of the content after a crucial step has already been taken. He also dislikes the inevitable feeling of never knowing enough. "And what I really like least about my work," he says, "is the solitude and focus required to prepare for the parts I like best."

Earnings

Jim uses a number of methods to charge for his work. He tries to generate at least $50 to $75 per hour, but may sign on for a flat project fee and agree on a fixed number of hours up front.

For a video project, he may charge $100 to $450 per finished minute of the script. This refers to the number of minutes the finished video will be and includes all of the research and rewrites. His advantage in writing video scripts is knowing what will and won't be expensive to shoot.

Jim says, "Starting out, you should take what you can get. Experience and learning are everything; money is nothing. Eat salad."

Advice from a Professional

Jim's first advice to aspiring technical writers is, "Don't fake it!" He feels that the only way you become competent and therefore valuable is to start out as incompetent. Don't pretend to know what you don't, but don't be afraid to take on challenges and work extra hours. Make up for inexperience with enthusiasm. Seek out people who are better than you, no matter how good you get.

Jim feels there is a myth that technical writing does not require creativity. On the contrary, all good communication requires creativity. He believes that placing the content within the context of a story is essential to comprehension and retention. To put your point across, you need to establish a context or a framework in which the information is functional.

"The only real joy in work is doing something you love and getting good at it," Jim says. "If I were just starting out, I would look for work in the marketing department of a small company, ad agency, or PR firm. You will get a wide range of experience in various media and be required to generate copy for everything from brochures to ad copy to instruction manuals."

KATHLEEN FROST
Documentation Specilist
Kathleen Frost works for Magnet Communications, Inc., an Internet banking software company in Atlanta, Georgia. She has been in the field since 1985 and has learned much of what she knows on the job. She also participated in a proposal writing and technical editing program at Southern Tech in Atlanta.

Getting Started

Kathleen had written four published articles and also tried writing fiction. She was shocked and pleased to learn that she could write well and get paid for doing something that came easily to her.

For her first technical writing job, a company was willing to take a chance based on Kathleen's writing ability. They trained her in their method of writing self-paced training materials and sent her to work in a nuclear power plant in Homestead, Florida. She got her current position because she had enough variety in her previous contracts to fit all the company's needs as the only documentation person in a small, fast-growing firm. Her background also proved that she was capable of taking on the management position when the company was ready to hire more people in the documentation department.

The Realities of the Work

Kathleen specializes in computer and software documentation and training and says that she always thinks of technical writing as translating the computerese practiced by programmers and technical people into the everyday English needed by a customer to use the product.

As a technical writer, she must be able to identify with the product users because it is they who see the product from the application side, not the planning and programming side. Fortunately, more companies are realizing how important good documentation is to a salable, profitable product.

The writer must be the user representative, helping to plan the user interface, making sure labels, screen, and button actions are consistent, so the user won't get lost. The writer also plans the product library, to give users the information they need in an easy-to-use format. In the end, the users only see a screen and the manual or online help, and their impression of the application is only as good as these two pieces. They are not interested in the length or cost or number of lines of code written. If the product doesn't work as advertised, users become frustrated and sometimes angry, and the company loses its word-of-mouth advertising and repeat sales.

Kathleen's company works with high-profile banks who buy Magnet Communications products and sell the associated services to their corporate clients. Magnet's contracts state that the product comes with online help and documentation. More and more customers are asking to see samples of the documentation that will go to them and to the end users. Many also want to know how to customize the help and documents with their logo and preferred colors, before they even buy the product.

Documentation is a big selling point for Kathleen's company. She writes online help for both the bank and end-user services, large product manuals that describe all the services with that product and how to set them up, and manuals on concepts that cover multiple products. She also prepares technical documents for installation and support, programming reference manuals, and some marketing overview material.

Kathleen's schedule varies depending on how soon the next product release is scheduled. She often answers requests, either directly from a customer or one passed on from the customer relations manager or a customer service representative. At other times, she works on a manual, interviewing the programmers or product managers to determine how the product works and what to tell the user.

The Upsides and Downsides

Kathleen finds her work interesting because she always has something new to do. The office is very fast paced, and she is busy verifying and editing all the documentation done before she arrived, as well as writing help and overviews for all the new services as they are developed.

She enjoys the opportunities to work with the application in the test environment, suggest user-related changes in the interface, and point out whether labels and actions are consistent. She is often also involved in final testing and quality assurance. In addition, Kathleen likes the strong team environment that allows her to participate in everything from initial planning to the final testing and release notes. She also is able to telecommute 50 percent of the time.

What Kathleen likes least are jobs where she has only one set product and has to write revisions for the same manual over and over for consecutive releases. "This kind of job can be so boring," she says, "you look for a new position to do something different."

Advice from a Professional

Kathleen's advice includes some options for aspiring technical writers. She points out that while some companies ask for degrees, others prefers years of experience—but the route you take to this career will depend on a few factors.

You might consider one of the many colleges that offer courses and degrees in technical communication. On the other hand, you might pursue the option of building real-world experience, but this might involve taking low-paying jobs and is not feasible for everyone. You also might work part-time, doing freelance work to build experience, or take classes at night—either of these options show potential employers that you are willing to work at your craft.

Kathleen's other suggestions include brushing up on your grammar and punctuation skills by taking a class in editing, posting your name to do ghostwriting or editing at a local college, and joining Internet newsgroups or mailing lists that will give you ideas. Many of these groups post job opportunities, and although you won't be ready for most of the jobs at the beginning, you should read the postings carefully, along with all job listings on the various newspapers and job websites. Find ones you would like to do someday and read the qualifications. Determine how you can get experience in those areas to someday qualify for your dream job.

As with any other freelance job, Kathleen recommends that you write whenever and whatever you can. Volunteer to do work for any organization or church you might belong to. Tell everyone you meet what you do and what you're looking for, and take a chance whenever you can—you never know what opportunities networking might lead to.

Once you get a job, learn everything you can. Offer to learn the new applications so you can teach the others in the group, then put the new application and the ability to teach it on your résumé. Offer to take a programming course with the developers so you can learn to read the code and write the manuals and technical installation documents they need—and then put the programming language on your résumé.

Kathleen also recommends joining the STC. This will allow you to post their membership plaque in your work area to let others know you're serious about your profession. It is well worth the yearly dues, and many companies will pay them for you. Get permission to submit your best manual to an STC competition. Everything you do and accomplish should go on your résumé.

In summary, Kathleen says, "Enjoy the benefits and take the risks. I was the first one to volunteer when many years ago a company I was working for sold an application to a bank in Hong Kong. The bank wanted the software customized for them, and that included the documentation. I was lucky enough to spend nearly a year in Hong Kong, with an apartment, utilities, and a per diem paid by the client. You never know where a solid, portable skill such as technical writing can take you."

THREE HELPFUL TIPS

Here are some tips to keep in mind as you prepare for a career in technical writing:

• Be prepared to work hard to learn a variety of applications; this will give you a broad background and enhance your chances for success.

• Take advantage of opportunities to volunteer or participate in internships as a means of gaining experience.

• Once you've gotten a job, learn as much as you can and do extra work when you can. This will get you noticed when opportunities for advancement arise.

C H A P T E R

8

MARKETING, ADVERTISING, AND PUBLIC RELATIONS WRITING

"Most writers regard the truth as their most valuable possession, and therefore are most economical in its use."

—Mark Twain

Writers are invaluable to the fields of marketing, advertising, and public relations, which all use the written word as the backbone of their enterprises. To the uninitiated, these areas might seem to be more similar to each other than not, but there are distinct differences:

• Marketing writers are hired to help create a "concept"—the initial introduction to the client's message—and marketing strategy, and then use the written word to communicate that concept to specific audiences.

• Advertising copywriters craft advertising copy for use by publications or broadcast media (radio and TV) to promote the sale of goods and services. They work closely with marketing personnel.

• Public relations writers must avoid much of the hype that is more freely employed by advertising writers. While an ad writer can sing the praises of a product or company, a PR writer must get the message across more subtly. Companies pay to have their advertisements run; PR writers try to place stories and press releases as features and editorials, not as advertisements.

Let's take a more in-depth look at each of these three areas.

MARKETING AND ADVERTISING

Although advertising and marketing are distinct fields, they are often linked together. (Some definitions peg marketing as the broad category that encompasses advertising as well as other disciplines, such as public relations and sales.) In simple terms, advertisers create a package to sell a product, service, or idea; marketing experts help target the audience to which the advertising should be aimed.

The goal of advertising and marketing is to reach the consumer—to motivate or persuade a potential buyer; to sell a product, service, idea, or cause; to gain political support; or to influence public opinion. To help achieve this goal, marketers poll public opinion and analyze the demographics and buying patterns of specific audiences. They play the roles of researcher, statistician, social psychologist, and sociologist.

With an idea of the specific audience to target, advertising professionals assess the competition, set goals and a budget, design an advertisement—whether a simple three-line ad or a full-blown campaign—and determine the best way to reach that audience.

JOB TITLES

In smaller agencies, departments can be combined or services contracted out to independent subcontractors. In most large advertising agencies, however, the organizational structure includes the departments of agency management, account management, creative services, traffic control and production, media services, publicity and public relations, sales promotion, direct response, television production, and personnel.

Advertising agencies employ a number of professionals to perform a variety of duties in each of these departments. Selected job titles are described here.

Agency Manager

In a small agency, the manager could be the president, the owner, or a partner. In large agencies, the manager could be the chief executive officer reporting to a board of directors or an executive committee, much as in any corporation. The agency manager is responsible for establishing policies and planning, developing, and defining goals to ensure growth and economic viability.

Account Manager/Executive

An agency's client is usually called an *account*, and the account manager supervises all activity involved with a specific account and is ultimately responsible for the quality of service the client receives.

The account manager functions as a liaison between the advertising agency and the client's organization. He or she must be thoroughly familiar with the client's business, the consumer, the marketplace, and all the aspects of advertising such as media, research, creative design, and commercial production.

Small agencies might function with just one account manager; large megaagencies could have hundreds, each handling a number of accounts. Account managers usually reach their position after working up through the ranks.

Assistant Account Manager/Executive

The assistant account manager generally reports directly to an account manager and can be assigned a wide range of duties. Some of these duties include analyzing the competition, writing reports, and coordinating creative, media, production, and research projects.

Most people working in this position have at least a bachelor's degree. Although a specific major in advertising or marketing isn't a prerequisite, most agencies look favorably on communications majors.

Account management departments, along with media departments, hire the greatest number of entry-level candidates. Entry-level positions in advertising often quickly lead to more senior roles.

Creative/Art Director

The creative department of an advertising agency develops the ideas, images, words, and methods that contribute to the ultimate product—the commercial, ad, or campaign. A variety of professionals work together in the creative department to meet the client's needs. The creative staff includes writers, artists, and producers, who work under the supervision of the art director from the initial campaign concept to its final production.

Competition is usually strong for entry-level positions in advertising creative departments. Having a good portfolio to present to the art director will be a plus. Submitting freelance work can also help you get a foot in the door.

Assistant/Junior Art Director

The assistant art director reports to one or more art directors and is usually responsible for preparing paste-ups and layouts for television storyboards and print ads. The assistant can also be involved in developing visual concepts and designs and supervising commercial production and photo sessions.

A two-year associate's degree from an art or design school is a very good way to enter this position. Agencies also like applicants who have a bachelor's degree with communication skills and strong graphic arts experience. Even more important than your degree, however, is having an excellent quality portfolio that displays skill and creativity. The most successful applicants for this position are those with some related experience such as an internship or practicum spent in a retail advertising department or another related setting.

Copywriter and Assistant/Junior Copywriter

Copywriters write body copy for print advertising and develop promotional materials. Their work might range from creating names for companies and products to writing television commercial dialogue or scripts for radio spots, to writing copy for direct-mail packages. Junior copywriters assist the copywriter as well as edit and proofread.

Applicants with the best portfolios are often selected over those with more education, but a bachelor's degree in communications, English, journalism, advertising, or marketing is certainly a plus. Even though some of the largest advertising agencies offer copywriting training programs, opportunities are limited for those with no writing experience.

Print Production Manager and Assistant

The staff of the print production department is responsible for the final creation of the advertisement. After the creative team has specified the different elements it wants incorporated into an ad, the print production team must see to it that the instructions are followed. They are responsible for two-color, four-color, and black-and-white printing, color separations, and the preparation of mechanicals. The print production department works closely with the traffic department and the creative staff, and it is also responsible for quality control.

Most agencies prefer applicants with some experience with production work. Although this isn't considered a highly competitive area, it is still a good place to break into the advertising business and move up to other positions.

Assistant Media Planner

The media department is responsible for making sure the advertising is presented to the right audiences, at the right time, and in the right place. As mentioned earlier, media departments are usually open to hiring entry-level candidates.

The assistant media planner reports to a senior planner and is responsible for the following duties:

- Gather and study information about people's viewing and reading habits
- Evaluate programming and editorial content of different media vehicles
- Calculate reach and frequency for specific target groups and campaigns
- Become completely familiar with the media in general as well as specific media outlets
- Become well acquainted with media data banks and information and research sources

Media Buyer

Media buyers and their assistants keep track of where and when print space and air time are available for purchase. They verify that agency orders actually appear or run and calculate costs and rates. They are familiar with all media outlets and have strong negotiation skills.

These professionals also have excellent communication skills, possess strong general business skills, and are able to work under pressure. They are also adept at working with numbers and are familiar with basic computer programs such as spreadsheet software.

Candidates for entry-level positions are expected to have a bachelor's degree and to exhibit a facility for working with numbers and spreadsheet software. Some large agencies offer training programs for new hires.

Traffic Manager and Assistant

The traffic department makes sure that various projects are conceived, produced, and placed as specified. The manager and staff are responsible for scheduling and record keeping. For those with more interest than experience, this is an excellent place to get a foothold in the industry.

Market Researcher

Professionals working in market research departments are tuned in to the consumer—what he or she worries about, desires, thinks, believes, and holds dear. Market researchers conduct surveys or one-on-one interviews, utilize existing research, test consumer reactions to new products or advertising copy, track sales figures and buying trends, and become overall experts on consumer behavior.

Agency research departments can design questionnaires or other methods for studying groups of people, implement the surveys, and interpret the results. Sometimes research departments hire an outside market-research firm to take over some of the workload. For example, a market researcher could come up with a procedure to test the public's reaction to a television commercial; the outside firm would put the procedure into action. Most people working in this field have at least a bachelor's degree, although many have earned master's degrees in marketing or other areas of business.

Assistant Research Executive

Assistants report directly to a research executive and are responsible for compiling and interpreting data and monitoring the progress of research projects. They must have strong quantitative skills and an aptitude for analyzing data. Computer skills and the ability to write and speak effectively are also essential.

Although a bachelor's degree is the basic requirement, it is becoming more common to find master's degree and Ph.D. holders in this field. A graduate of a college program that emphasizes research would have an edge on the competition.

Publicists

While advertising is written exactly the way the client wants and is placed where he or she hopes it will have the most impact, the writing and placement of publicity is determined by the staff of the media (TV and radio stations, newspapers, and so forth) to which it is sent. All media outlets have the option to rewrite press releases or even ignore them. When used properly, however, publicity provides free advertising for products, services, and events.

When it comes to promotion, clients and business owners have more control. They stage events, organize activities, and print and distribute promotional materials. Here are a few examples of the way publicity and promotion work:

- A professional athlete endorses a brand of athletic shoe (for a fee, of course).
- A television talk-show host invites the author of a new book to be a guest on the program.
- A publisher arranges a book-signing tour to promote an author's new book.
- A soap opera star promotes community service programs.
- A professional association imprints its name and logo on tote bags to be given away at its annual conference.
- A political candidate reads a ghostwritten speech at a rally.
- A television magazine show explores a breakthrough cure for cancer.
- A vacation resort entices travel writers to visit.
- A beer company sponsors "BeerFest" at a sporting event.
- A "guerrilla marketer" stands on the street corner and thrusts free samples of a product into the hands of passersby.
- Someone wearing a Big Bird outfit stands in front of a new store, inviting passersby to enter.

The professionals in charge of organizing these promotional activities are called publicists or PR people. Although they work in a variety of settings and have a wide range of duties, the most important thing they have in common is that they are all excellent communicators. They are also creative and have extensive knowledge of and contact with the media.

PUBLIC RELATIONS

Public relations specialists serve as advocates for such organizations as businesses, governments, universities, hospitals, and schools, working to build and maintain positive relationships with the public. As managers recognize the growing importance of good public relations to the success of their organizations, they increasingly rely on public relations specialists for advice on strategy and policy of such programs.

The organizational functions handled by PR specialists include media, community, consumer, and governmental relations; political campaigns; interest-group representation; conflict mediation; or employee and investor relations. However, public relations involves much more than simply "telling the organization's story." Understanding the attitudes and concerns of consumers, employees, and various other groups is also a vital part of the job. To improve communications, public relations specialists establish and maintain cooperative relationships with representatives of community, consumer, employee, and public-interest groups as well as those in print and broadcast journalism.

Those who work in public relations put together information that keeps the general public, interest groups, and stockholders aware of an organization's policies, activities, and accomplishments. Their work keeps management aware of public attitudes and concerns of the many groups and organizations it must deal with.

The PR department prepares press releases and contacts people in the media who might print or broadcast their material. Many radio or television special reports, newspaper stories, and magazine articles start at the desks of public relations specialists. Sometimes the subject is an organization and its policies toward its employees or its role in the community. Often the subject is a public issue, such as health, nutrition, energy, or the environment.

Public relations workers also arrange opportunities for contact between organization representatives and the public. For example, they set up speaking engagements and often prepare the speeches for company officials.

They represent employers at community projects; make film, slide, or other visual presentations at meetings and school assemblies; and plan conventions. They are also responsible for preparing annual reports and writing proposals for various projects.

PR specialists who work in government are also called press secretaries, information officers, public affairs specialists, or communications specialists. They keep the public informed about the activities of government agencies and officials. For example, public affairs specialists in the Department of Energy keep the public informed about the proposed lease of offshore land for oil exploration. A press secretary for a member of Congress keeps constituents aware of their elected representative's accomplishments.

Those who handle publicity for an individual or who direct public relations for a small organization may deal with all aspects of the job. They contact people, plan and perform research, and prepare material for distribution. They may also handle advertising or sales promotion work to support marketing.

Some public relations specialists work a standard thirty-five- to forty-hour week, but unpaid overtime is common. In addition, schedules often have to be rearranged to meet deadlines, deliver speeches, attend meetings and community activities, and travel out of town. Occasionally they have to be at the job or on call around the clock, especially if there is an emergency or crisis.

IN-HOUSE OR FREELANCE

Writers in marketing, advertising, and public relations have a choice: work in-house for an agency or firm as a full-time employee or build up a client list and work as a freelancer. You'll see from the firsthand accounts at the end of this chapter that most freelancers have gained a solid background by working first for advertising or PR firms before striking out on their own.

As in any field, there are advantages and disadvantages to both situations. Full-time employees have the security of a regular paycheck and benefits, but not much say in the projects they work on. Freelancers have to scramble for new clients, at least when first starting out, and never know exactly how much money they'll earn from month to month. On the other hand, once established, freelancers can pick and choose the projects that interest them.

POSSIBLE EMPLOYERS

A variety of employers require the talents of advertising, marketing, and PR specialists. Keep reading if you are interested in full-time employment in these fields.

Advertising Agencies

More than 425,000 people were employed by advertising agencies in 2004, and an additional 61,000 were self-employed. Although advertising agencies are located throughout the United States and Canada, they are concentrated in the major cities. California and New York together account for about one in five firms and more than one in four workers in the industry. Although firms vary in size, ranging from one-person shops to international agencies employing thousands of workers, 68 percent employ fewer than five people.

You don't have to live in New York or California to find a successful career in advertising. Young and Rubicam has grown from a successful advertising agency into a leading market communications company, with 163 agencies in 81 countries. In the United States, they have offices in Chicago, Detroit, Irvine, Miami, New York, and San Francisco. The company's Canadian offices are in Calgary, Halifax, Montreal, Toronto, and Vancouver.

Advertising agencies help clients to identify potential customers, create effective ads, and arrange for the air time or print space to run the advertising. Large agencies generally have a wide range of clients and can be a tremendous source of experience for a new graduate. Starting in a small agency would allow graduates to quickly specialize in a particular area of advertising.

Marketing Firms/Departments

Since marketers and advertising professionals work hand in hand, many marketing departments are located within corporate advertising departments or in private advertising agencies. Private marketing firms function similarly to advertising agencies and work toward the same goals of identifying and targeting audiences that will be receptive to specific products, services, or ideas.

Corporate Advertising Departments

Although many corporations use the services of outside advertising agencies and marketing firms, just as many, especially the very large ones, operate their own in-house departments. In these settings, workers create and develop the company's advertising and sales promotion material. For example, the professional staff of a large department store such as Macy's or Sears will create catalogs, brochures, newspaper inserts, and flyers, as well as place the regular flow of daily newspaper ads.

Developing these materials, especially glossy catalogs, is a big endeavor that requires the skills of a variety of people, including copywriters, art directors, photographers, layout artists, and modeling agencies.

Corporations that use the services of an outside agency might also maintain their own advertising department to function as a liaison between the agency and the client company. Here the responsibilities include ensuring that the advertising meets the company's objectives and is placed in the appropriate media outlets.

Publishing Companies

Large publishing companies, especially those located in New York City, operate publicity departments to promote their authors and their books. These publicists arrange for point-of-sale material (for example, printed bookmarks) to be made available at bookstores; organize book tours, including speaking engagements on television and radio shows and book-signing engagements at bookstores and other appropriate outlets; and write book jacket copy.

Bookstores

More and more bookstores, especially the superstores such as Borders and Barnes and Noble, coordinate events to bring in the customers. This calls for a publicist who can book big-name and local authors for speaking and signing engagements, arrange for cookbook authors to give cooking demonstrations, and find other ways to appeal to the tastes of the book-buying public.

Vacation Resorts/Chambers of Commerce

Promoting a vacation spot or a city falls into the realm of a publicist's duties. Publicists working for a vacation resort produce pamphlets, brochures, press releases, and video demonstrations and Web-based material to showcase the location's selling points. Their target audience includes travel agents, travel writers and editors, and the vacationing public. Publicists working for Chambers of Commerce aim their efforts at potential businesses and new residents, as well as vacationers and other visitors.

TRAINING

The most suitable course of study for potential advertising or marketing specialists has been the issue of some debate. There are those who believe that a straight degree in advertising or marketing is the best preparation, but they are usually shouted down by those who recognize the importance of a broader curriculum.

To some extent, the answer is determined by the career path you intend to pursue. If you hope to work as an account manager, courses in marketing, business and finance, and speech are as important as advertising theory. Potential art directors obviously need technical training in drawing, illustration, and graphic design. Regardless of your intended area of specialization, however, you will be well served by courses in effective communication—the ability to write and speak well is essential in every aspect of advertising and marketing.

Although there are no defined standards for entry into a public relations career, a college degree combined with public relations experience, usually gained through an internship, is considered excellent preparation for entry into the field. Many beginners major in public relations, journalism, advertising, or communications. Some firms look for graduates who have worked in electronic or print journalism; others prefer applicants with demonstrated communication skills and experience in a field related to the firm's business, such as science, engineering, sales, or finance, for example.

Essential skills include creativity, initiative, good judgment, and the ability to express thoughts clearly and simply. You'll also need to excel at decision making, problem solving, and research. As for personal attributes, you must be outgoing, be self-confident, understand human psychology, and be enthusiastic about motivating people. You should be competitive, yet flexible and able to function as part of a team.

Many large companies offer formal training programs for new employees. New employees in smaller organizations generally work under the guidance of experienced staff members. As a beginner, you will maintain files of material about company activities, scan newspapers and magazines for appropriate articles to clip, and assemble information for speeches and pamphlets.

After gaining experience, you'll write news releases, speeches, and articles for publication, or perhaps design and carry out a public relations program. Working in a smaller firm will give you all-around experience, whereas working in a larger firm will make you more specialized.

The Public Relations Society of America accredits public relations specialists who have at least five years of experience in the field and have passed a comprehensive six-hour examination (five hours written, one hour oral). The International Association of Business Communicators also has an accreditation program for professionals in the communications field, including public relations specialists. Candidates must have at least five years of experience in a communication field and pass a written and oral examination. They also must submit a portfolio of work samples demonstrating involvement in a range of communication projects and a thorough understanding of communication planning. Those who meet all the requirements of the program earn the designation Accredited Business Communicator. Employers consider professional recognition through accreditation a sign of competence in this field, and it may be especially helpful in a competitive job market.

CAREER OUTLOOK

The glamour and excitement of advertising and public relations should contribute to keen competition for jobs in these fields. Employment in the industry is projected to grow 22 percent through 2014, compared with 14 percent for all industries combined. New jobs should be created as the economy expands and generates more products and services to advertise. In addition, growth in the number and types of media outlets used to reach consumers should increase demand for advertising and PR services, creating opportunities for people skilled in preparing material for presentation on the Internet.

On the other hand, employment growth may be tempered by the increased use of more efficient nonprint media advertising, such as Internet or radio, which could replace some workers. Employment also may be adversely affected if legislation aimed at protecting public health and safety further restricts advertising for specific products such as alcoholic beverages and tobacco. Layoffs are common in agencies when accounts are lost, major clients cut budgets, or agencies merge.

On the management side, positions in advertising, marketing, and public relations management are highly coveted and will be sought by other managers or highly experienced professionals, resulting in keen competition. College graduates with related experience, a high level of creativity, and strong communication skills will have the best job opportunities. In particular, employers will seek those who have the computer skills to conduct advertising, marketing, promotions, public relations, and sales activities on the Internet.

Job opportunities for market researchers are expected to grow at the same rate as for managers.

THE JOB HUNT

As in the corporate world, it's a good idea to become a familiar fixture inside an advertising agency's main reception area. Sending out résumés blindly has never been an effective method for finding a job in most professions, and works even less frequently in these settings. The key is having a good portfolio with you, one you can quickly open and display if the right person takes an interest. A portfolio should showcase your best work and should be specific to the area in which you're applying. If you are interested in copywriting, visuals are less important than writing samples and a good marketing sense. Aspiring art directors need samples of their work that show their design ability. Persistence is a trait valued in these fields; showing the same quality in your job search can pay off.

Here are two tips to help you with your search:

- Start your job search before you near graduation. Arranging to participate in an internship at a company you'd like to work for will give you an edge. By becoming a familiar face at the company or agency, you'll be likely to be considered before an unknown applicant when a new opportunity arises.
- Learn as much as you can about the agency or firm you're interested in. In other words, target your prospects.

POTENTIAL EARNINGS

Your salary will vary depending on whether you work full-time or as a freelancer, among other factors.

Salaried Employees

There are conflicting reports on how much you can make, ranging from little to lots. It depends mainly on the agency and your position. According to a National Association of Colleges and Employers survey, in 2004 starting salaries for marketing majors averaged about $34,000; advertising majors, about $29,500; and public relations majors, about $29,700.

Median annual earnings for salaried public relations specialists were $43,830 in 2004. The majority earned between $32,970 and $59,360; the lowest 10 percent earned less than $25,750, and the top 10 percent earned more than $81,120.

People working for government, health-care, or nonprofit organizations generally earn less than those working for private, for-profit agencies and corporations. Most people increase their salary by changing jobs and moving from agency to agency. This is an industry where relationships and networking are crucial to a new position and more money.

Freelancers

Some freelancers charge an hourly rate for their work; others charge a flat fee per project. Some use both methods, depending on the project.

Here are some freelance writing areas that fall under advertising, marketing, and public relations, and the income average rates based on the 2006 *Writer's Market* survey:

Advertising copywriting	$84/hour	$2,400/project	$1.50/word
Book jacket copywriting	$67/hour	$315/project	$0.50/word
Campaign development or product launch	$77/hour	$4,250/project	n/a
Catalog copywriting	$83/hour	n/a	$60/item
Copyediting for advertising	$37/hour	n/a	n/a
Direct-mail copywriting	$78/hour $400/page	$2,725/project	$1.50/word

E-mail ad copywriting	$58/hour	n/a	n/a
PR for businesses	$70/hour	n/a	n/a
PR for government	$50/hour	n/a	n/a
PR for nonprofits	$52/hour	n/a	n/a
PR for schools and libraries	$50/hour	n/a	n/a

FIRSTHAND ACCOUNTS

Read the following accounts of professionals currently working in marketing, advertising, and public relations to see whether these fields might be right for you.

JOAN CAMENSON
Advertising Copywriter

Joan Camenson has an associate's degree in fashion merchandising from the Fashion Institute of Technology, New York. She has more than twenty years of experience as an advertising copywriter with a specialty in retail advertising. She works for the in-house advertising department for Stage Stores, a large retailer specializing in apparel, accessories, cosmetics, and footwear for men, women, and children. They have more than six hundred stores in thirty-three states; their corporate headquarters is in Houston, Texas.

Getting Started

While she was majoring in merchandising, Joan chose an elective in advertising copywriting. She found that she loved the course material and discovered that she had a talent for writing, which led to a decision to pursue it as a career. Since she was changing majors from merchandising to writing, Joan wasn't able to get any assistance from her school's placement office. She was determined, however, and found a job by making cold calls to employers in New York City.

When she applied for her current position, Joan initially responded to an ad for a writer. She had an interview but didn't get the job. Three months later the copy director called to offer her a more senior position as staff writer, and she accepted the job.

The Realities of the Work

Joan does retail writing for direct-mail catalogs, inserts and statement enclosures, and newspaper ads. She receives fact sheets from the store's buyers and studies the merchandise to write copy that will persuade customers that they need to buy the item. She also attends "turn-in" meetings, in which merchants present the items they've purchased for a particular season or ad. To stay current on trends, Joan relies on trade papers and the Internet for information.

Joan submits an ad to the copy supervisors for correction, and it then appears in proof form. At this stage the ad shows the text and photography elements. The merchant approves the ad or requests changes or corrections.

The Upsides and Downsides

What Joan likes most about her job is the writing and the ability to interact with the staff of buyers. She is busy most of the time and gets to regularly interact with people at all stages of the advertising process.

On the downside, the decreasing number of retail stores means that there are limited advancement opportunities. She has tried repeatedly to advance to a management position but has not been successful. In addition, Joan would like to see more of a team effort and collaborative discussions about how to work on specific projects.

Advice from a Professional

Based on her own experience, Joan advises others interested in advertising writing to get as much exposure as possible to different types of writing. She cites her own lack of experience in radio and television writing as a mistake in her career.

Joan also recommends learning as much as possible about print media and the Internet, which will make you more competitive in a shrinking market. She says, "When I started out, there were lots of retail organizations, all with their own advertising departments, and so there were lots of opportunities to find jobs. Today, that is not the case. Stores are swallowing up other stores, and you have a much more limited area to work."

If you major in writing or journalism, Joan encourages you to minor in a subject that you like so that you can learn to write about it. "I remember meeting a nurse who was an editor for a nursing magazine," she says. "She had majored in nursing and had a minor in writing. She was able to successfully combine both of her interests. If I had it to do over again, I would have tried to find out about becoming a travel writer or a food writer."

MARINA RICHARDS
Advertising/Marketing Writer

Marina Richards has worked in a variety of advertising agencies as a full-time copywriter. Currently freelancing, she writes print ads, radio and TV scripts, website content, brochures, and direct response materials. She has a B.A. in advertising and has been in the field for twenty years.

Getting Started

Marina was interested in combining her business acumen with her love for creative writing, and she was excited about the opportunity to work with interesting people in different fields.

The summer after college graduation, Marina applied for a writing/editing position at her local ABC television affiliate. Because this was a highly sought-after position, she didn't think she had much chance of success, but she decided to pursue the job anyway. The director of advertising invited her for an interview and instructed Marina to bring her portfolio. Although she was thrilled to get the interview, she was panicked because she didn't have a portfolio.

Marina recalls that she spent a week scrambling to put together a portfolio of writing and concept samples. She suddenly felt that all of her work from college looked amateurish, and lacking drawing skill, she cut photos and other visuals from magazines and carefully glued them to her art boards. She explains that she was attempting to show a basic sense of layout and design as a copywriter.

Her work paid off, because Marina was asked for a second interview where she was introduced to the general manager and given a tour of the station. After three weeks of waiting, she was offered the job.

Marina worked for ten years in advertising agencies, television stations, and in-house corporate departments. After building up her experience, she decided to strike out on a freelance career and now works from home.

The Realities of the Work

Marina says that when projects are slow, agencies are very laid-back and casual. This all changes, however, when projects abound and the agency is under pressure to meet deadlines. She has worked around the clock on high-profile projects, and describes a sample job for us.

A project might come from a client who needs a direct response brochure to introduce a new telecommunications package to business-to-business customers. The copywriter is briefed on the marketing strategy by the account executive and art director, and this becomes the guide for how the writers will proceed with the project.

The copywriter and the art director start by "concepting"—coming up with ideas for the product. They look through old design magazines and study the client's competition as well as any other materials they can find related to similar products.

Marina likes to ask clients to show her a campaign they loved, which she finds is a very good way to gauge the client's taste. She then tries to determine what tone the copy should reach for—formal, informal, highbrow, conversational. It's important for a successful copywriter to be able to write in many different voices.

Once the copy is written based on the agreed-upon concept, it is read by the creative director, who usually makes constructive comments that are addressed by the writer. While all this is going on, the account executive is regularly checking in with the staff, asking about their progress.

The copywriter and art director present the visuals and written copy to the account executive and marketing director. Marina describes this as "a panicky moment. Think politics here. The senior account executive and the marketing director could be a problem if they don't like your concept."

If the executives do like the concept, they and the copywriter discuss how to present the materials to the client. Marina says that this stage often involves working all night to prepare for the presentation. The client comes to the agency, and the writer has no idea how many people will see the presentation.

Generally, the account executive makes a presentation and then introduces the writer, who shows the art board and talks about the concept. Marina stresses the need to be interesting and to add value to the client's product. The writer should anticipate questions and be prepared to explain why the concept will work for the client's strategy. If the concept isn't accepted, the team goes back to the drawing board.

When the client does like the concept, the writer polishes the copy until it is ready for print. Sometimes the account executive instructs the copywriter to develop additional material, such as brochures or ads, to go with the initial brochure. At this point, the project has become a full-blown advertising campaign that will take a month or more to complete.

Once the copy is approved, the art director and designer begin working on the project, and the writer has some down time before jumping back into the mix. For the writer, the next stage is receiving "blue-lines," which is when the layout and copy are typeset. The writer gets one final look at a proof of the copy to ensure that the printer didn't miss anything or make an error.

"And that's it," Marina says. "Your brochure, the baby you've been nurturing, the creative concept that you drew from your head and onto paper, is done. When the finished product arrives, you grab a few for your portfolio."

The Upsides and Downsides

For Marina, one of the best things about her work is the opportunity to work with creative and intelligent people. She also loves being paid to be creative, as well as having the possibility of winning awards for one's work. She cautions, however, that the field is very competitive and the award-winning ads are truly deserving of the recognition.

On the downside, many things can go wrong during an ad campaign. After all the work, the client might not like the concept, and the pressure can be overwhelming.

Earnings

When she worked as a copywriter for a large Boston advertising agency, Marina earned $62,000 a year. She says that a senior writer would earn more, depending on the geographic location and size of the agency.

Marina's fee as a freelancer is between $60 and $75 per hour, depending on the project.

Advice from a Professional

Marina recommends getting a bachelor's degree in English, advertising, communications, or journalism. Assemble a portfolio and use it to make contacts and get interviews and job offers.

You should be innovative, be able to think for yourself, and not be afraid to ask questions. You should also have a sense of irony, creatively speaking, but hokey or cornball humor is not what creative directors and others look for. You must be able to write and come up with smart ideas. As Marina says, "You don't have to be brilliant, but you should make others think you are!

"It can be a cutthroat business. But once you have enough experience, you can take your samples and go just about anywhere and make a living."

SUSAN DITZ
Public Relations Writer

Susan Ditz is the owner of SMD Communications, a marketing communications, public relations, and editorial services concern in California. She writes applications, trend and success stories, newsletter pieces, and Web content, in addition to press kit materials such as fact sheets, backgrounders, white papers, and brochures. She also writes company and executive profiles that she places in the *Business Journal*, and she ghostwrites features for executives. She also works as a contractor for several PR agencies on special projects. She has a B.S. in journalism from Boston University and has been working in the field for more than thirty years.

Getting Started

After graduation, Susan worked as assistant editor for a weekly newspaper group in Massachusetts. When the paper was sold, she heard about a small agency that needed help, and she managed to get a job as account executive by stretching the truth about her PR training, which in fact was nonexistent. To Susan's advantage, the boss had just landed a major account and was fairly desperate for an assistant, so the job was hers.

Her new boss taught Susan how to write a proper press release, develop a television script, produce a TV show, write an advertorial, and manage events. Once she had gained some experience, she realized that she could make more in PR than as a junior staffer on a paper, so she moved on to a bigger agency in Boston. In this job, Susan worked on PR for McDonald's, Nabisco, PUCH Mopeds, and Dexter Shoe. In addition to press kits, she prepared cause-related marketing materials and wrote newsletters and brochures.

After working in the agency and both the corporate and nonprofit sectors, Susan decided to start consulting. As a single mother, she wanted to have a much more flexible schedule and to stop commuting, and she saw consulting as an excellent way to achieve this goal.

The Realities of the Work

Susan describes her work as very diverse. She has worked for clients in health care, nonprofit, computer software, hardware and peripherals, telecommunications, wine and food, restaurants, shoes, bicycles, real estate, marine products, and sporting goods. Simultaneous projects include writing content for a website, developing two feature stories, preparing a marketing plan for a nonprofit group, and planning long-range publicity for several entertainers.

Susan says that because effective PR depends on being proactive and innovative, she scans industry publications and websites to stay on top of emerging trends or potential problems. Her days generally begin with strategic management, which includes making decisions and setting priorities. The rest of the day is spent executing the plan, developing one for the next day, and managing e-mail. The workday doesn't end until the work is finished, which typically takes about twelve hours.

As a consultant, Susan both writes on assignment and develops her own ideas. Opportunities arise all the time, so new business is not hard to find. Her days are basically ruled by deadlines as she tries to complete all of her current projects.

Susan says that working on her own requires that she is good at juggling work. She often has four to six projects going simultaneously, but she likes to work this way and is never bored. However, there are times when the amount of work can be daunting. She once spent two months working eighty-hour weeks with almost no breaks on a contract job that went far beyond the original deadline, because she had another project that she was also committed to complete.

On the flip side, there have been months when projects have stalled and no money was coming in. Susan says, "These are the times I start buying lottery tickets, or wishing I'd gone to law school. It usually gets me looking furiously at websites and classified ads for a full-time position. But then the phone rings and I'm taking notes for a proposal."

The Upsides and Downsides

On the positive side, Susan enjoys the potential for interesting adventures and the chance to learn new things by working with bright, creative people.

The down side is that the job includes a lot of stress. Working with the media and keeping up with communication technology can also involve a good deal of frustration.

Earnings

Susan reports that although her salary fluctuates somewhat from year to year, she earns in the mid- to high five-figure range. She says that starting salaries in her field vary depending on where you live. In Silicon Valley, where Susan is located, salaries are quite high, but so is the cost of living.

Advice from a Professional

Susan recommends that you take advantage of every opportunity to intern in agencies, nonprofits, and corporations while still in school. Before embarking on a PR career, get some experience working in the news business. If you think you want to work in the corporate world, do so for a while before investing in an M.B.A. And read a lot.

NEWMAN MALLON
Public Relations Writer
Newman Mallon is director of marketing for Identicam Systems Canada, Ltd., a distributor of photo identification and Smart Card technology. He has a bachelor of applied arts in radio and television arts from Ryerson Polytechnical Institute in Toronto, and a bachelor of journalism from Carleton University in Ottawa.

For our purposes, he discusses his time as a self-employed public relations consultant and writer.

Getting Started

After studying radio and television arts, Newman worked for five years as an audiovisual technician for a school board. Although this was good training, he noticed that a lot of PR or media relations jobs advertised required a journalism degree. He knew he liked writing after having taken three radio and TV writing courses, so he decided to take a one-year program in journalism at Carleton University for graduates with a good writing portfolio.

Newman's first job in the field came through a referral from a professor. He was later able to get into a self-employment program sponsored by the unemployment insurance commission, which supplied a weekly living allowance to start his own business.

The Realities of the Work

The writing that Newman did in his own business was largely high-tech as well as industrial, financial, and business-to-business. His projects included corporate backgrounders, speeches, press releases, PR planning, and feature and ghostwritten articles.

Newman explains that in most agencies, PR writers are called account executives and are liaisons to the client. They write the copy for press releases, corporate backgrounders, feature articles, speeches, and proposals. In an agency that also offers integrated marketing communications, the PR writer may also write brochures, invitations, mailers, moving notices, or even audiovisual presentations.

The clients a PR writer deals with will vary from agency to agency. For example, if the agency specializes in high tech, the writers may work on business software in the morning and computer games in the afternoon. If it's a consumer-related agency, it could be hair mousse one hour and motorcycles the next. Consulting, PR planning, idea or story angle development, research, writing, revisions, and approvals are all part of the job.

In most cases, the writer comes up with his or her own ideas for editorial pieces that will suit the publication. The copy must be informative or interesting to readers of the publication. Newman explains that unlike advertising, where a writer can play up the client and products, editorial material should be done without much hype about the client company. Basically, PR writing includes a mention of the client's name, a review of its product, a business success story, or some quotes from a spokesperson. This keeps the company name in the news.

When a PR writer is planning which editors or publications to approach for a campaign, it is best to look for those that already appeal to the client's target audience or those who might buy the company's product. Next, the writer looks for editorial features that have something to do with the product or industry, and develops a story or informative piece to fit that feature issue, which is then pitched to the editor. Often, the publication will want its own staff writers to actually write the piece. If that is the case, the PR writer can set up any interviews they need and provide them with information about the company.

Newman warns that the job can be very hectic with trying to find new clients, pitch stories to editors, and research and write articles or news releases that editors will print. Often, clients do not understand the need to write for the editor, or may require a lot of hand-holding and explanation. Clients also don't realize how long it takes to pitch and write a good editorial piece.

When he ran his own business, about 60 percent of Newman's time was spent on administrative details and marketing his own services. The rest was writing and consulting or billable work.

The Upsides and Downsides

Newman says that this business is full of ups and downs. It can be very stimulating when projects are on the desk and work is flowing, but routine when the work is slow and he has to find clients.

The work requires a lot of time, sometimes as much as fifty-five hours a week, so there's little opportunity to take time off. This is especially true when a writer is juggling several projects at once.

Advice from a Professional

Newman's advice to aspiring PR writers is to gain whatever experience you can by writing for smaller publications, and then work your way up to develop a portfolio. This will show that you can write for the press. Even volunteer work can add up to experience that will help you land that first job.

Strong written and verbal communication skills are mandatory. You should also be diplomatic and able to work well on your own as well as in a team environment. Newman also suggests that any knowledge of a specific industry you've worked in previously will help you land that first job, if your prospective employer has a client in that industry.

BOB MANSKER

Former Deputy Public Printer of the United States

Bob Mansker worked for many years as a press secretary for former Congressman Martin Frost from Texas. He holds an M.B.A and Ph.D. in business administration.

Getting Started

Bob says that although he was always fascinated by reporters, he didn't want to follow the traditional journalism path of working for newspapers, television, or radio. But his journalistic interest, combined with an interest in politics, provided the perfect background for a career as a press secretary.

He began by volunteering for local political campaigns, writing press releases and newsletters, becoming familiar with the political process, keeping on top of current events, and making a lot of contacts. When Congressman Martin Frost, Democrat from Texas, won his first seat in the House of Representatives in 1979, he moved to Washington, D.C., and Bob moved with him.

Working on political campaigns and during a stint in the state legislature, he gained an insight into the needs of a political organization for written and oral skills in the radio and television media. He also learned how to write press releases and newsletters for various members of Congress.

The Realities of the Work

Bob wrote press releases on the Congressman's position on a multitude of issues. These releases were then sent to different media with the hope that the information would be printed or aired.

He also wrote a weekly newspaper column and produced *Martin Frost Reports*, a monthly newsletter on a variety of issues for the voters in the district. He produced radio and television programs, scheduling the Congressman in various studios, and met regularly with media representatives from newspapers, magazines, and television and radio stations.

Three or four times a year Bob traveled to the congressional district in Texas to remain acquainted with local media. He also made occasionally trips abroad, including accompanying the Congressman to Russia and visiting the Middle East.

The Upsides and Downsides

For Bob, one of the best things about the job was the regular interaction with people who are constantly keeping aware of national and world events and who have a respect for the political structure and makeup of the political electorate of the nation.

On the down side, the work was fully dependent on the Congressman deciding to seek and win reelection. Bob says that the job can also be repetitious at times, but he sees this as a factor of most jobs.

Bob worked as press secretary to Congressman Frost for fourteen years, after which Frost appointed him Staff Director of the Accounts Subcommittee, Committee on House Administration. Congressman Steny H. Hoyer of Maryland named Bob to the Joint Committee on Printing staff in 1995. In September 1997 Bob was appointed Deputy Public Printer of the United States, the second highest position in the U.S. Government Printing Office. He held this position until 2003.

Advice from a Professional

Bob acknowledges that a college degree is not a necessity for a career as a press secretary. Someone with a sound knowledge of their home state, a good command of English, and an understanding of the political organization could be hired. However, he warns that most employers would wonder why the applicant had not earned a degree. Finishing college will give you an edge over other candidates.

He feels that practical experience campaigning is valuable, as are any studies in general communications. Writing and organizational skills are crucial, and some understanding of the media is also helpful.

Overall, though, Bob advises that the well-rounded applicant stands the best chance of winning the job. He says, "If you come to apply for one of these positions, we aren't just going to look at your writing or journalism ability. We're going to look at you as a person."

MARCUS GRIMM

Radio Copywriter

Marcus Grimm is a marketing strategist from Lancaster County, Pennsylvania. He has published fiction writing in a variety of magazines and nonfiction in several of trade magazines, and he has written advertising slogans for in-store displays for such stores as Linens & Things, AMES, and Sears. He has a B.A. in communications from Elizabethtown College in Elizabethtown, Pennsylvania, and is the winner of the 2004 Central Pennsylvania Writing Contest.

Marcus worked for three years in Hershey, Pennsylvania, as the production coordinator for WRKZ-FM, a 50,000-watt country station. He wrote everything from advertising copy to press releases, corporate video scripts to newsletters.

Getting Started

Since Marcus has always loved both radio and writing, he felt that radio copywriting was the perfect job to allow him to blend his two interests.

While taking a college professional-writing class, he had an assignment to interview someone doing a job that he would like to do. He called the largest local radio station and got an interview with the creative director, who was impressed with Marcus's portrayal of him. Marcus volunteered to do some writing for the director, and later served an internship at the same radio station. When the internship ended more than a year later, he was offered a paying job to do the same work.

The Realities of the Work

The radio station employed about twelve different sales representatives, each of whom would bring in a copy sheet that detailed what the client was trying to sell on the radio. Clients ranged from lawyers and doctors to car dealers and owners of farmers markets, so their advertising needs were varied. The copy sheet might indicate how the client wanted his or her company or products portrayed, or perhaps just the preferred tone of the ad.

Based on the copy sheet, Marcus would write a script and have someone voice and produce the ad. Next he would either play the spot over the phone for the client or give a cassette copy to a sales representative to play for the client in person.

Marcus wrote sixty-second scripts. Some focused on making the audience aware of the advertiser's services, while others highlighted special products or sales. Although the subject matter was up to the client, Marcus generally selected the theme, which is what he says will make or break an ad.

Marcus found working at a radio station to be exciting, because it is an instant medium in which ads may air literally within minutes of being written and produced. He also believes that they provide a good training ground for developing writing skills. In his own experience, he has found that he wouldn't write a story because he couldn't form all of the elements properly. But in radio copywriting, most of the elements, such as characters and setting, are provided, and the writer must fill in the blanks. Also, because radio is, in Marcus's words, "the theater of the mind," there are no real rules to follow. He once wrote an ad about a truck driving through a wall of eggs—in television, this would have been a very expensive project, but for radio, it was free.

The workweek never exceeded forty hours, which Marcus attributes to the professionalism of the creative director, who valued quick and effective copywriting. And there were occasional celebrity sightings as well, since musicians who came to town to play concerts would often stop by radio stations to thank them for playing their music.

The Upsides and Downsides

Marcus enjoyed the wide variety of personalities working in radio, since so many creative and intelligent professionals work in this field. He also appreciated the wide variety of writing styles he got to practice daily. Another plus was the satisfaction he felt each time he heard one of his commercials on the air.

The greatest downside for Marcus was that the money was not there, and this is what eventually made him leave the business. Because copywriting is considered an expense in radio, stations do whatever possible to keep the pay low.

The only other downside he mentions is understanding that the commercial is owned by the client. This means that no matter how wonderful or inventive a writer's idea is, if the client doesn't love it, the idea won't go anywhere.

Earnings

Marcus says, "I got into radio by offering my services for free, and if you have the ability, that's probably the easiest way to get in, as it's a very competitive business. Eventually I was paid $6 per hour. The day I decided to get out of radio was when I found out that after twenty years in the business, the creative director at our station was making only $28,000 per year.

"In the radio business, pay is often relative to station and market size, and I was working for the largest station in our market. Since I wasn't looking to move, I realized that my pay would not likely ever exceed my boss's."

Advice from a Professional

Based on his own experience in radio copywriting, Marcus offers three words of advice for those interested in this career: "Volunteer. Volunteer. Volunteer."

He believes this is the best way to gain entry into the environment of radio and to see what the industry is all about. He also recommends listening to commercials aired by different stations to see which are the most creative, since some copywriters are far ahead of their peers in terms of creativity and imagination.

To succeed in this field, Marcus cautions that you must appreciate the needs of a business in order to write a creative ad around it. You must also be able to handle criticism from clients and salespeople, and remember that the client's desires must always come before your own.

"Finally," Marcus says, "understand that unless you're happy making less than average money, radio copywriting will probably serve as an extremely enjoyable stepping stone to an advertising agency or more lucrative position elsewhere. Still, appreciate it for what it is.

"In the words of my old boss, 'Radio is the ultimate dream world. We've got cowboys that never rode a horse and guitar players who never held a pick.'"

THREE HELPFUL TIPS

To launch a successful career as an advertising, marketing, or PR writer, keep these tips in mind:

• Unlike most of the other writing careers you've read about in previous chapters, writers in these fields don't write about their own ideas. Instead, they work for clients who provide the ideas and must be able to adapt to the clients' wishes. You'll have to be able to write in a variety of styles and on a range of topics, depending on the needs of the client.

• Working at an agency is a very good place to begin. Even though you may have to start at the bottom, you'll gain valuable experience and learn how the industry works. This experience will be invaluable if you decide to work for yourself later on.

• If you are freelancing, use whatever resources you can to expand your client base. Use the Internet or your library's out-of-state telephone directories to locate new business prospects, or place advertisements in related publications to make your services known to clients outside your immediate area.

C H A P T E R

9

OTHER OPPORTUNITIES FOR WRITERS

"I would sooner read a timetable or a catalogue than nothing at all."
—*W. Somerset Maugham*

Career writers don't just write books or articles for magazines and newspapers. And there are many avenues to pursue other than technical, advertising, or public relations writing. Some permit (or require) full-time employment; others allow for freelancing independence.

Here's a list of writing or writing-related job titles that fall under the category of other opportunities for writers:

Agent	Ghostwriter
Blogger	Greeting Card Writer
Book Reviewer	Newsletter Writer
Comedy Writer	Reader
Contest Judge	Résumé Writer
Copyeditor	Speechwriter
Critic	Writing Instructor/Lecturer

AGENT

Many agents begin their careers in publishing houses, working as editors with a particular genre or two. They begin to work as agents to have more freedom with the type of books they'll handle. Many agents are also writers and know what the industry is like from both sides of the fence.

Some of the bigger literary agencies, which are mostly in New York City, hire assistants and provide training until you can be promoted to associate status. Agents with more experience in publishing might immediately start their own agency after a stint at a publishing house.

You should be aware that some agents with no experience also strike out on their own. They have few contacts with publishers, are not familiar with what types of projects different editors are seeking, and often charge fees to writers for their services, above and beyond the usual commission. Writers are strongly warned to avoid these agents. A successful agent must build a good reputation based on well-earned experience.

Contact the Association for Author's Representatives (AAR) for more information on becoming an agent. Their address and website are provided for you in Appendix A.

BLOGGER

Bloggers write for the Internet, mainly writing personal reflections on subjects of close personal or professional interest. Some blogs take the form of a personal diary; others read like reports from the field—firsthand, subjective accounts of an event or an activity. Most are written for recreational reasons with little expectation of earning a fee; however, some blogs promote a business or support a cause and may generate interest or income through other activities.

The growing popularity of blogs could allow some writers to get their work read; a few well-written blogs may garner some recognition for the author and may lead to a few paid pieces in other print or electronic publications. However, most bloggers don't earn much money from their endeavors.

There are exceptions, of course. One example is Julie Powell, whose blog titled *The Julie/Julia Project* chronicled her culinary adventures as she cooked her way through every recipe in Julia Child's book *Mastering the Art of French Cooking*. The blog was a huge hit, and Julie subsequently got a book deal from Little, Brown and Company. Her book, *Julie and Julia: 365 Days, 524 Recipes, 1 Tiny Apartment Kitchen*, was published in 2005.

BOOK REVIEWER

Most large newspapers and some magazines and newsletters feature book sections. Although many of the book reviews are written by the book section editor or staff writer, some publications will accept freelance work.

To get your foot in the door, you can obtain a copy of a book you would like to review, read it, then write your review and send it in. Newspapers in different regions of the country do not compete with each other, so you could sell a single review to more than one market.

If you make a sale, the next assignment will be easier to come by, and you'll be given a comp copy of the book you are going to review.

Another option is to simply query a book editor first, before writing the review. The editor might provide you with a comp copy or expect you to get your own. If the latter is the case, you can contact the publisher of the book you'd like to review with a request for a review copy. Many publishers are quite generous with their comp copies and ask in return only that you send them a copy of the review when it is printed.

Your query might produce an assignment, or at least an agreement to look at your review on spec. Querying first will also let you know if the book you have chosen has already been reviewed.

COMEDY WRITER

Can you combine your writing ability with a strong sense of humor and quick wit? Are you naturally funny and instinctively able to make others laugh? If so, you might find your niche writing comedy routines and gags for stand-up comics or jokes for people who have to speak in front of an audience. You might even find yourself on a writing team for Jay Leno or Conan O'Brien.

Contact comedians (hang out in comedy clubs and see how approachable they are) or speakers bureaus, and offer your services. The rates you could expect to receive are listed later in this chapter.

CONTEST JUDGE

Most judges for well-known writers' contests are usually well-established agents, editors, or authors. This is not an area for an unknown to find work.

Judges are usually assigned specific categories, such as short-story entries or romance novels, and then given a number of entries to read, sometimes critique, and judge.

COPYEDITOR

Some publishers rely on the services of freelance copyeditors to proof and mark up manuscripts to get them ready for typesetting and printing. You have to be a stickler for detail to be comfortable with this type of work. You also must be familiar with the type of editorial notations you'd find in *The Chicago Manual of Style*, for example. Approach publishers with a letter and résumé.

CRITIC

Look in the back pages of any magazine geared toward writers, and you'll see a slew of ads placed by critics, manuscript evaluators, and "book doctors." You can place one there, too.

A good critic must have an understanding of what makes fiction or nonfiction publishable, know how to point out strengths and weaknesses, have a good command of grammar and structure, and be an articulate report writer.

Good critics also know never to promise publication or agent representation upon completion of their critique and a rewrite by the writer. This type of false advertising has had state attorneys general investigating and punishing these improper practices.

GHOSTWRITER

Ghostwriters write books for people who don't have the necessary skill to do it themselves. Clients could be famous personalities such as former presidents or movie stars who want to tell a story. They could also be self-publishers or experts in a particular field who have topics they want to see in print but don't have the time, skill, or experience to do it themselves.

Ghostwriters sometimes get credit for their writing (you might see "as told to" on the book jacket cover), but they often remain anonymous, writing behind the scenes.

Landing a ghostwriting job for a celebrity is not an easy task, unless you know someone who can help you make the right contacts. Publishers generally assign these books to writers they have worked with in the past.

But this doesn't mean that a writer with credits and some tenacity couldn't approach a celebrity with a pitch something along these lines: "As a writer interested in [celebrity's specialty], I have faithfully followed your career since [date of the celebrity's first accomplishment]. I know you have a story to tell, and I would love to help you tell it. I haven't seen your autobiography in bookstores yet, but it's a book I know publishers—and the public—would be interested in." Who knows, it could work . . .

Ghostwriting for a self-publisher is the easiest way to establish credits, but you still need to proceed with caution. Often self-publishers have already written a book that they haven't been able to sell to a publisher. They might want you to rewrite the book or add your name as coauthor to lend credibility to the project. You'll get paid when you sell the book.

Other self-publishers might have what they consider to be a hot idea that they are sure would be a bestseller if only they had the ability to write the book. They want you, the ghostwriter, to write it for them and submit it to publishers, and they will pay you whatever you want—out of the huge advance they're sure the book will merit.

In both situations, most professional writers would simply say no. Professionals know how difficult it is to sell a book, and if they are going to have to wait until it sells to be paid, they might as well continue working on their own books.

Contacting book packagers (listed in the *Literary Marketplace*) with your résumé, writing samples, and stated availability and areas of expertise could possibly land you a contract. For example, a book packager has just been assigned a travel book on South Africa. You have just come back from a six-month tour there. And your letter happens to arrive just as the packager is wondering who he could possibly find for this project. Being in the right place at the right time can go a long way. And it does happen.

GREETING CARD WRITER

We all spend a lot of time in front of racks of greeting cards, looking for the perfect way to say "Happy Birthday" or "Get Well Soon." In fact, it seems that the greeting card section of most stores has grown considerably in recent years, as more and more occasions become part of our world. So-called ethnic holidays, foreign-language cards, Grandparents' Day—someone writes those greeting cards and gets paid fairly nicely for such a small number of words. Greeting card publishers usually will look at several ideas at once, buy all rights, and pay either upon acceptance or upon publication. You can find greeting card publishers and information on how to submit to them in the most recent *Writer's Market*.

NEWSLETTER WRITER

Most organizations, from big-time corporations to small nonprofits and charities, put out newsletters. These can be aimed at a variety of audiences, including staff, members, stockholders, donators, neighborhood residents, clients, customers, and potential customers.

The focus and content of newsletters vary depending on the audience and the activities of the organization. They could range from news on the health-care industry to stock tips, to a listing of potential markets for freelance writers to approach.

Some newsletters are available at no charge to subscribers and are sent through e-mail or regular post; others charge a subscription fee or depend on advertising—or both—to cover expenses.

Depending on the size and budget of the organization, some newsletters are generated in-house; others are contracted out to freelance writers and editors. Newsletter writers might provide all or part of the content, or they might depend on contributions from staff or other outside freelancers. Some newsletter writers are solely responsible for layout, proofreading, editing, and printing; others report to an editor and work with graphic artists and typesetters.

Writers find jobs writing newsletters through classified ads, through online databases, by contacting organizations directly, through word of mouth, and sometimes through internships and by volunteering.

It is rare that one newsletter would provide enough income to support a writer, so most freelancers who specialize in newsletters have contracts with more than one organization, or they also do other types of writing.

You'll learn more about being a newsletter writer through a firsthand account later in this chapter. See also Chapter 4 for a breakdown of the article-writing process.

READER

You may have seen advertisements stating that you can earn money just by reading and screening books for publishers or agents. The advertiser—for a fee—will show you how to land these plum jobs. The next time you see one of those advertisements, keep turning the pages. Most of these offers are scams. Agents and editors either do their own reading or delegate it to junior-level assistants.

RÉSUMÉ WRITER

Job seekers need résumés and you can find work writing and updating them. Résumé writers can work for employment agencies or they can freelance, leaving business cards at print shops and advertising in newspapers, career magazines, and online.

Résumé writers must be familiar with the different résumé and curriculum vitae formats, including the requirements for electronic submission. They must be able to listen to their clients in order to pull out the appropriate information, and they must know how to tailor each résumé to the specific type of job being sought. In addition, good résumé writers know how to translate a client's experience into "résumé-speak," so that even a new graduate with little experience can look like a qualified applicant for an entry-level position.

SPEECHWRITER

Speechwriters work with politicians and other public figures, listening to what they want to say, researching the issues, and writing the speeches they will deliver. When you see the president on television or hear the mayor or governor speaking to a group of voters, you can be pretty certain the speech was written by someone else.

Political speechwriters find work through word of mouth and contacts, sometimes through classified ads, but mostly by volunteering in campaigns and getting themselves and their work noticed.

Speechwriters can be employed full-time for an elected official, or they might follow different candidates over the years from campaign to campaign. They can also be paid by the project.

You'll learn more about being a speechwriter through a firsthand account later in this chapter.

WRITING INSTRUCTOR/LECTURER

The old adage, "those who can, do; those who can't, teach," doesn't apply here. The best writing instructors are those who are good writers themselves and can offer constructive criticism to students.

Writing instructors work in colleges and universities. They also work for adult education programs, or they are hired to speak and conduct workshops for various writers' organizations or conferences. Some organize their own workshops and seminars, renting classroom or hotel space, or meeting in their own homes. Still others conduct classes online, either via e-mail or through Internet chat rooms.

To make your services known, take the following steps:

- Conduct an Internet search for online (as well as off-line) writing programs.
- Contact local writers groups such as state chapters of Romance Writers of America or Mystery Writers of America.
- Visit local bookstores and offer to speak on a subject of interest to writers, in addition to sitting for a book signing.
- Contact your local library and offer to do a series of workshops for writers.
- Apply to the adult education programs offered by universities, community colleges, and school boards.
- Organize your own seminars: rent a mailing list (*Writer's Digest* is a good source), rent a meeting room, decide on topics, print up brochures, and mail them out.

POTENTIAL EARNINGS

The following table is a breakdown of the payment you can expect for a variety of writing jobs not covered in previous chapters. The information is from the 2006 *Writer's Market* survey, which is updated every year. For a more complete listing, consult the most recent *Writer's Market*.

FIRSTHAND ACCOUNTS

Read the following accounts of professional writers who have made a career in these other writing areas. Perhaps one of these fields is right for you.

Table 9.1   Breakdown of Average Wages for Various Careers

Job Title	Wages
Agent	15 percent commission from the sale of a client's work to publishers; some charge 20 percent for foreign and movie rights
Book reviewer	$133 per project; $0.44 per word
Comedy writer	for nightclub entertainers, $38 per joke; $250 per routine
Copyeditor	for magazines, $32 per hour; for advertising, $37 per hour; for book publishers, $29 per hour, $4.10 per page; for Web pages, $44 per hour
Critic	for book queries, $40 per hour, $300 per project; for poetry manuscript, $85 per hour; for short story manuscripts, $55 per hour; for novel manuscript, $46 per hour, $840 per project
Ghostwriter	for magazine articles, $100 per hour, $2,880 per project, $1.08 per word; for business (trade magazines), $100 per hour, $750 per project, $1.00 per word; for a book (as told to), $60 per hour, $25,000 per project; book (uncredited), $69 per hour, $29,778 per project, $1.00 per word
Greeting card writer	$125 per card
Newsletter writer	for a four-page newsletter, $64 per hour, $2,000 per project, $2.00 per word
Résumé writer	$100 per project
Speechwriter	for a general 30-minute speech, $81 per hour, $5,480 per project; for government officials, $76 per hour, $4,500 per 20-minute speech; for political candidates, $92 per hour, $650 per 15-minute speech
Writing instructor	college course or seminar/adult education, $70 per hour, $2,260 per course, $367 per day; for workshops, $75 per hour, $324 per event

POLLY STARNES

Media Relations Consultant/Speech Writer

Polly Starnes has worked as an advertising copywriter for radio, TV, and print; a technical writer; a public relations writer; and a political media relations consultant. In this firsthand account she focuses on the twelve years she spent as a speechwriter for various politicians.

Polly has a degree in communications from Loyola University, New Orleans, with a minor in political science.

Getting Started

When Polly was a child, her family was involved in Louisiana politics. As she grew older, she realized that although she wasn't interested in holding office, she was fascinated by the campaign process. The science of persuasion represented both a great challenge and the power of the media to influence voters.

Polly once wrote a political television commercial for a candidate who was running far behind the incumbent in the polls. Her commercial ran only once on the three major networks because the incumbent threatened to sue his opponent's campaign. This turn of events reversed the campaign and Polly's candidate won the race by a landslide. After this experience, she was hooked on media relations.

Early in her career, Polly was writing copy at a radio station when she was approached by a political operative who asked if she was interested in taking a leave of absence to work on a governor's race. She was asked to write position papers, print pieces, and speeches for education and union members. She decided to take a chance, figuring that her job would be waiting when the campaign ended.

After the governor's race, Polly began to buy media for the congressman from her district and to write copy for his print and electronic ads. As her work increased and her reputation grew, she began spending more time in Washington, D.C., than in Louisiana. Polly moved to the capital based on her reputation for being able to write in a style that built up her clients while subtly attacking their opponents.

The Realities of the Work

Polly's work involved interacting with politicians running for office or reelection. She wrote position papers, sometimes called "white papers," reflecting the candidate's stand on a particular issue, how he or she would improve the situation, and how it would work to improve the lives of constituents.

She also wrote speeches directed toward specific interest groups such as environmental, education, and labor unions, as well as speeches for small gatherings where a candidate would meet new people in his or her district. When the candidate was occasionally called away to attend another function, Polly would deliver the speech herself.

Polly describes speech and political writing as being about dialogue—how to assemble the dialogue of what people want to hear in a manner that they will understand. She stresses the importance of never writing down to the listener, combined with the ability to write and deliver a speech as though the listener knows nothing about the subject. Speechwriters walk a fine line between keeping listeners engaged and not making them feel inadequate or ignorant.

Polly's clients were Democratic candidates for public office. She wrote speeches for Tony Knowles, governor of Alaska, during his campaign for mayor of Anchorage; former Louisiana Governor Edwin Edwards; former U.S. Senator Phil Gramm, while campaigning as representative; and former U.S. Representative Charles E. "Buddy" Roemer. She also wrote the speech that President Ronald Reagan delivered at the initiation of the Ringling Bros. and Barnum & Bailey Circus's Safe Kids Program.

Although most of Polly's speech writing was directed toward professional educators and union members, her work also included any position that the candidate needed to address, such as environmental reform.

Polly points out that if a speechwriter has been with a campaign since the beginning, she has probably contributed to writing the position papers. This would mean that the writer is familiar with the candidate's stand on issues and would have ready access to most, if not all, of the research on a given topic.

She acknowledges that it can be difficult to discover exactly what the opponent's stand is, and here research is an important factor. Speechwriters need to be good detectives, working to find out what the opposition is printing in his or her position papers, as well as what the opposite camp is saying to its supporters. This might involve attending public meetings where the opponent is speaking and interviewing supporters for comments. Polly says that by doing this, you can reach not only your client's supporters, but also voters who are undecided—you might even persuade people away from the other candidate through your investigation, strategy, and sharp writing skills.

During campaign season, speech writing is a round-the-clock job, and speechwriters are at the mercy of the candidate and the campaign. Polly has been called in at 2:00 A.M. to write or rewrite a speech needed to answer an attack the opposition made during the 10:00 P.M. news. A speechwriters must always stay in tune with what is going on and be alert for information about the client—whether it's overheard in a restaurant or on the evening news. Knowing how to listen and how to act on information you gather is vital.

Flexibility is a must for working on a campaign, particularly in speech writing. It might be necessary to revise a talk as the candidate walks to the podium to speak, based on a comment that was just broadcast on the news.

Good speechwriters must also be fund-raisers, including an appeal for money at every opportunity. This is very important, since it is the funds raised by the campaign that pay the writer's salary.

Polly advises that a speechwriter must be a PR person when traveling with the candidate—answering questions and knowing when to say "I don't know that answer but will get it and get back to you." Remember that following through is important, because supporters depend on what they are told. The ability to think quickly and not say the wrong thing are key factors. You must be energetic, congenial, and never tired, and be willing to do anything at any time.

And as for traveling, Polly stresses that a speechwriter must be able to board an airplane at a moment's notice and be willing to buy clothes at the destination, since you probably won't have been home long enough to do the laundry or pick up your dry cleaning. But you'll mingle with heads of state and domestic workers, people of all ages and backgrounds, and you must be able to understand their needs.

One of the most important things to keep in mind is that there is no room for error in this job. A speechwriter must be able to organize and delegate and must choose the right person for each job. Mistakes can cost a candidate's office, reputation, and money, and might even lead to legal problems.

Once the November election is over, most speechwriters have nothing to do until March or April. Many use this time to pay attention to who the candidates will be in the next election and to plan their strategy for landing a contract with the candidate they hope to work for.

Polly warns that it isn't a good idea to try to work with a candidate for money only. "To write about things you do not firmly believe in will not work," she says. "Business is business, but conscience is conscience." She speaks from experience, having once written a speech denouncing the ERA when she is a firm supporter of the movement. She became angry, and even developed physical ailments as a result of writing what she didn't believe. Since Polly was a good friend of the candidate, she chose to leave the campaign rather than lose a friend over the issue.

The Upsides and Downsides

On the positive side of the job, Polly talks about the excitement as being key to enjoying the position, coupled with the challenge of persuading others to believe in what you believe.

Polly says that time off between campaigns can be good or bad, depending on a person's situation. She always enjoyed it because she was able to spend all of her time with her son. Other speechwriters use the down time to travel or to rest. But she cautions that you must be a good money manager to make sure that you can survive these months without any income.

Earnings

Polly says that each campaign is structured differently, and her fee was dependent on the size of the campaign, local or national. She usually worked on salary, from a few thousand to upward of $90,000 per campaign, depending on her degree of direct involvement.

Polly has written single speeches for $300, and has written fund-raising speeches for a percentage of what was contributed. There are as many ways to structure your fee as there are campaigns.

Advice from a Professional

Based on her extensive experience, Polly has some sound advice for aspiring speechwriters. "You must be adaptable and willing to do anything at any time," she says. "Speechwriters might have to pitch in with a campaign, for example, and find themselves doing telephone solicitation if the volunteers don't show up.

"You need a strong interest in making the world a better place and have ideals that you would like to see met. You may have positions on certain issues that you would like to see changed, so you become involved in the campaign and grow within a network of people."

Polly suggests starting as a campaign volunteer and doing as much as you possibly can in that position. Your contributions will be noticed, and you'll be rewarded for your input.

In addition to education, Polly believes that a successful speechwriter also needs talent, personality, discipline, and an insatiable curiosity for ferreting out facts to enhance your candidate. "A good political media relations person needs to be a good PR person as well as a good writer," she says. "This is not just a writing job."

CARMA SPENCE-POTHITT
Newsletter Writer

Carma Spence-Pothitt is editor of *The Genre Traveler* (http://thegenretraveler .com), an e-zine devoted to the travel-related interests of readers of science fiction, fantasy, and horror. The e-zine has just finished its first full year and is doing well. For the purposes of this book, however, Carma talks about her work as editor and writer of the member, producer, and employer newsletters for Blue Shield of California.

Carma has a bachelor's degree in biology from the University of California, Santa Cruz, and an M.A. in journalism from the University of Maryland, College Park. She has been working in this field for nearly fifteen years and has also worked in public relations.

Getting Started

Carma has been writing fiction and poetry since childhood, and she also loves science. While she was studying biology in college she took a science writing course that gave her direction for her future. She worked in customer service to save money for graduate school, where she pursued her simultaneous love of science and writing.

Based on a recommendation from her advisor, Carma applied for a writing position with the Maryland Agricultural Experiment Station while still attending graduate school. She enjoyed writing about the work of the scientists, and she also knew that this job would be a good starting point for a career.

The Realities of the Work

Carma's particular subspecialty at Blue Shield was publications, and although she generally worked with newsletters, she might also be involved with brochures, magazines, or flyers. She saw a publication from conception to print, which is an ongoing task with periodicals, as she was often working on several issues at the same time.

Carma worked on writing eight separate newsletters: three published three times a year, four published four times a year, and one bimonthly. She describes the biggest challenge as trying to remain calm when others don't meet deadlines. Her work ran on deadlines, and missing one affected all of her projects.

Carma's main writing responsibility was light health-care stories and business updates. Story ideas usually came from an editorial board or from material she read that she thought would interest her audiences. Sometimes her supervisor or manager mandated a story.

On a typical day, she read and responded to a large number of e-mail messages, discussed potential problem situations over the phone, and then found the time to write. Each day was different, but the most fulfilling were those she was able to spend writing and editing.

Carma usually worked more than forty hours a week. She says that newsletter writing has many highs and lows and, depending on the specifics of the job, can sometimes be stressful. "The more responsibility you have, the more fun and challenging the job can be, but the more stressful it can get," she says.

The Upsides and Downsides

What Carma loved most about writing a newsletter was turning raw material into a final publication. She says, "I get a lot of satisfaction from seeing a Word file turned into a newsletter or magazine."

The most difficult aspect of the work was dealing with coworkers who don't fully understand her job and who ultimately impact the final product. She mentions those who don't understand the importance of meeting a deadline, or who change the copy at the final review stage without realizing that making extensive changes can cost a lot of money.

Earnings

When she started at Blue Shield, Carma earned $20,000—which was $5,000 less than she'd been making before she went to graduate school. By the time she left the company, she'd moved up to a salary of $45,000.

She says that beginners should expect to start around the midtwenties. This can grow rapidly as you gain experience, but that usually means changing companies rather than expecting pay raises.

Advice from a Professional

"Do what you love, and everything else will follow," Carma advises. "You have to follow where your passion leads you, or you're going to be very unhappy in whatever you do, but especially in this kind of high-stress job."

To succeed in newsletter writing, she recommends that you have talent in communication—writing, speaking, and interpersonal skills. A degree in marketing, journalism, or public relations will provide good training. If you plan to specialize in a particular field, such as science-related writing, a degree in that area will also be helpful.

Carma suggests that you work at building up your portfolio. For example, if you want to work as a marketing writer, volunteer at a nonprofit organization to build up your writing samples. Every time you apply for any kind of writing job, you'll be asked to provide samples, and it won't matter whether you got paid to do them, as long as they are high-quality work.

THREE HELPFUL TIPS

Here are some tips that can help you in whichever area of writing you decide to pursue.

• Don't be afraid to try different types of writing, at least until you've established your career. Most of the professional writers profiled throughout this book have done a variety of writing, from books to articles to newsletters to press releases. The more flexible you are, the more experience you'll gain, and the more likely you'll be to have a successful writing career.

• Pay attention to your craft; hone and polish your work until it shines. In the beginning, the quality of your work will be much more important than the quantity. Professional, quality writing will speak for itself.

• Be persistent. You know by now that rejection is a big part of becoming a published writer. Try not to be overly sensitive to it, and don't give up. Use rejection and criticism constructively—the more you improve your craft and learn the ropes of the industry, the better your chances for success.

APPENDIX

PROFESSIONAL ASSOCIATIONS

The following professional associations provide all or some of the following services: career pamphlets, newsletters, preparatory courses, market listings, agent listings, job listings, conferences, and other professional information.

AGENTS

The Association of Authors' Representatives, Inc. (AAR)
P.O. Box 237201 Ansonia Station
New York, NY 10003
aar-online.org

The website contains information on working as an agent as well as on working with agents.

BOOK PUBLISHING

American Booksellers Association
828 South Broadway
Tarrytown, NY 10591
bookweb.org

American Society of Indexers
   (ASI)
10200 West 44th Avenue, Suite 304
Wheat Ridge, CO 80033
asindexing.org

Association of American
   Publishers (AAP)
50 F Street NW
Washington, DC 20001
publishers.org

Association of American
   University Presses (AAUP)
71 West 23rd Street
New York, NY 10010
http://aaupnet.org

The Association of Canadian
   Publishers
161 Eglinton Avenue East,
   Suite 702
Toronto, ON M4P 1J5
publishers.ca

The Audio Publishers Association
audiopub.org

Authors Registry
31 East 32nd Street, 7th Floor
New York, NY 10016
authorsregistry.org

Canadian Booksellers Association
789 Don Mills Rd., #700
Toronto, ON M3C 1T5
cbabook.org

Canadian Publishers' Council
250 Merton Street, Suite 203
Toronto, ON M4S 1B1
pubcouncil.ca

International Publishing
   Management Association
710 Regency Drive, Suite 6
Kearney, MO 64060
ipma.org

National Association of
   Independent Publishers
111 East 14th Street
Zeckendorf Towers
New York, NY 10003
naipr.org

National Association of Publisher
   Representatives
54 Cove Road
Huntington, NY 11743
naprassoc.com

Publishers Weekly
publishersweekly.com

MAGAZINES

Council of Literary Magazines and
   Presses
clmp.org

Magazine Publishers of America
810 Seventh Avenue, 24th Floor
New York, NY 10019
magazine.org

Magazines Canada
425 Adelaide Street West,
	Suite 700
Toronto, ON M5V 3C1
magazinescanada.ca

Society of National Association
	Publications
8405 Greensboro Drive, #800
McLean, VA 22102
snaponline.org

MARKETING, ADVERTISING, PUBLIC RELATIONS

Advertising Photographers of
	America, Inc.
27 West 20th Street, Suite 601
New York, NY 10011
apanational.com

Advertising Research Foundation
432 Park Avenue South
New York, NY 10016
arf.org

American Advertising Federation
1101 Vermont Avenue NW,
	Suite 500
Washington, DC 20005-6306
aaf.org

American Association of
	Advertising Agencies
405 Lexington Avenue, 13th Floor
New York, NY 10174-1801
aaa.org

American Marketing Association
250 South Wacker Drive,
	Suite 5800
Chicago, IL 60606
marketingpower.com

Association of National
	Advertisers
708 Third Avenue
New York, NY 10017-4270
ana.net

Graphic Arts Information
	Network
200 Deer Run Road,
Sewickley, PA 15143
gain.net

National Council for Marketing
	and Public Relations
P.O. Box 336069
Greely, CO 80633
ncmpr.org

Point-of-Purchase Advertising
	Institute
popai.com

Promotion Marketing Association
257 Park Avenue South, 11th Floor
New York, NY 10010
pmalink.org

Public Relations Society of
America (PRSA)
33 Maiden Lane, 11th Floor
New York, NY 10038-5150
http://prsa.org

Publishers Marketing Association
pma-online.org

The Society for Healthcare
Strategy and Market
Development
shsmd.org

NEWSPAPERS

Accrediting Council on Education
in Journalism & Mass
Communications
University of Kansas School of
Journalism
Stauffer-Flint Hall
1435 Jayhawk Boulevard
Lawrence, KS 66045-7575
www2.ku.edu/~acejmc

American Society of Media
Photographers
150 North Second Street
Philadelphia, PA 19106
asmp.org

American Society of Newspaper
Editors
11690B Sunrise Valley Drive
Reston, VA 20191-1409
asne.org

AP Broadcast News Center
1825 K Street NW, Suite 800
Washington, DC 20006
apbroadcast.com

Association for Education in
Journalism and Mass
Communication
234 Outlet Pointe Boulevard
Columbia, SC 29210-5667
aejmc.org

Canadian Media Guild
144 Front Street West, Suite 300
Toronto, ON M5J 2L7
cmg.ca

The Dow Jones Newspaper
Fund, Inc.
4300 Route One North
South Brunswick, NJ 08852
http://djnewspaperfund.dowjones.
com/fund

Investigative Reporters and Editors
138 Neff Annex
Missouri School of Journalism
Columbia, MO 65211
ire.org

National Newspaper Association
129 Neff Annex
University of Missouri–Columbia
Columbia, MO 65211
nna.org

National Press Photographers
   Association (NPPA)
3200 Croasdaile Drive, Suite 306
Durham, NC 27705
nppa.org

Newspaper Association
   of America
4401 Wilson Boulevard,
   Suite 900
Arlington, VA 22203-1867
naa.org

The Newspaper Guild
501 Third Street NW
Washington, DC 20001-2797
newsguild.org

Radio and Television News
   Directors Association
1600 K Street NW, Suite 700
Washington, DC 20006-2838
rtdna.org

WRITERS AND EDITORS

Agricultural Communicators of
   Tomorrow
http://gonact.org/INDEX.htm

American Association for the
   Advancement of Science
   (AAAS)
1200 New York Avenue NW
Washington, DC 20005
aaas.org

American Medical Writers
   Association (AMWA)
40 West Gude Drive, Suite 101
Rockville, MD 20850-1192
amwa.org

American Society of Journalists
   and Authors
1501 Broadway, Suite 302
New York, NY 10036
asja.org

American Translators Association
225 Reinekers Lane, Suite 590
Alexandria, VA 22314
atanet.org

Association for Business
   Communication
Baruch College
Box B8-240
One Bernard Baruch Way
New York, NY 10010
businesscommunication.org

Association for Computing
   Machinery's Special Interest
   Group on Documentation
   (ACM/SIGDOC)
1515 Broadway, 17th Floor
New York, NY 10036-5761
sigchi.org

Association for Educational
   Communications and
   Technology
1800 North Stonelake Drive, Suite 2
Bloomington, IN 47404
aect.org

Association for Women in
   Communications
3337 Duke Street
Alexandria, VA 22314
womcom.org

Association of Teachers of
   Technical Writing
attw.org

Authors Guild, Inc.
31 East 32nd Street, 7th Floor
New York, NY 10016
authorsguild.org

Canadian Authors Association
Box 419
Campbellford, ON K0L 1L0
canauthors.org

Canadian Poetry Association
331 Elmwood Drive, Suite 4-212
Moncton, NB E1A1X6
canadianpoetryassoc.com

Center for Information-
   Development Management
infomanagementcenter.com

Copywriter's Council of America
Linick Building
P.O. Box 102
Middle Island, NY 11953-0102
http://lgroup.addr.com/ccaprofile.
   htm

Council for the Advancement of
   Science Writing
P.O. Box 910
Hedgesville, WV 25427
casw.org

Council for Programs in Technical
   and Scientific Communication
   (CPTSC)
cptsc.org

Council of Science Editors
c/o Drohan Management Group
12100 Sunset Hills Road,
Suite 130
Reston, VA 20190
councilscienceeditors.org

Editorial Freelancers Association
71 West 23rd Street, Suite 1910
New York, NY 10010-4181
the-efa.org

Editors Association of Canada
502–27 Carlton Street
Toronto, ON M5B 1L2
editors.ca

Fiction Writer's Connection
fictionwriters.com

Health and Science
   Communications Association
39 Wedgewood Drive, Suite A
Jewett City, CT 06351
hesca.org

Institute of Electrical and
Electronics Engineers'
Professional Communication
Society (IEEE/PCS)
ieeepcs.org

International Association of
Agricultural Journalists
ifaj.org

The League of Canadian Poets
920 Yonge Street, Suite 608
Toronto, ON M4W 3C7
poets.ca

Mystery Writers of America
17 East 47th Street, 6th Floor
New York, NY 10017
mysterywriters.org

National Association of Black
Journalists
University of Maryland
8701-A Adelphi Road
Adelphi, MD 20783-1716
nabj.org

National Association of
Government
Communicators
201 Park Washington Court
Falls Church, VA 22046-4527
nagc.com

National Association of Hispanic
Journalists
1000 National Press Building
529 14th Street NW
Washington, DC 20045-2001
nahj.org

National Association of Home and
Workshop Writers
P.O. Box 12
Baker, NV 89311
nahww.org

National Association of Science
Writers
P.O. Box 890
Hedgesville, WV 25427
nasw.org

National Conference of Editorial
Writers
3899 North Front Street
Harrisburg, PA 17110
ncew.org

National Federation of Press
Women
P.O. Box 5556
Arlington, VA 22205
nfpw.org

National Writers Union
113 University Place, 6th Floor
New York, NY 10003
nwu.org

Novelists, Inc.
ninc.com

PEN American Center
588 Broadway, Suite 303
New York, NY 10012
pen.org

Playwrights Guild of Canada
54 Wolseley Street, 2nd Floor
Toronto, ON M5T 1A5
playwrightsguild.ca

Poetry Society of America
poetrysociety.org

Professional Writers Association of
    Canada
215 Spadina Avenue, Suite 123
Toronto, ON M5T 2C7
pwac.ca

Romance Writers of America
16000 Stuebner Airline Road,
    Suite 140
Spring, TX 77379
rwanational.org

Science Fiction and Fantasy
    Writers of America
P.O. Box 877
Chestertown, MD 21620
swfa.org

Société Québéçoise de la
    Rédaction Professionelle
    (SQRP)
61-3509, rue Hutchison
Montreal, QC H2X 2H1
sqrp.org

Society of American Travel
    Writers
1500 Sunday Drive, Suite 102
Raleigh, NC 27607
satw.org

Society of Children's Book Writers
    and Illustrators
8271 Beverly Boulevard
Los Angeles, CA 90048
scbwi.org

Society for Technical
    Communication, Inc.
901 North Stuart Street, Suite 904
Arlington, VA 22203
stc.org

Writers Union of Canada
90 Richmond Street East,
    Suite 200
Toronto, ON M5C 1P1
writersunion.ca

APPENDIX

B

FURTHER READING

The following is a brief listing of how-to books and directories that will guide you on your way to a career in writing.

COPYEDITING

University of Chicago Press Staff, eds. *The Chicago Manual of Style*, 15th ed. Chicago: University of Chicago Press, 2003.

QUERY LETTERS AND PROPOSALS

Cool, Lisa Collier. *How to Write Irresistible Query Letters*. Cincinnati: Writers Digest Books, 2002.
Larsen, Michael. *How to Write a Book Proposal*, 3rd ed. Cincinnati: Writers Digest Books, 2003.

MARKETING YOUR WORK

Blanco, Jodee. *The Complete Guide to Book Publicity*, 2nd ed. New York: Allworth Press, 2003.

Deval, Jacqueline. *Publicize Your Book: An Insider's Guide to Getting Your Book the Attention It Deserves.* New York: Berkley Publishing, 2003.

Poynter, Dan. *The Self-Publishing Manual: How to Write, Print, and Sell Your Own Book*, 15th ed. Santa Barbara, CA: Para Publishing, 2006.

FICTION

Gotham Writers Workshop, eds. *Writing Fiction: The Practical Guide from New York's Acclaimed Creative Writing School.* New York: Bloomsbury USA, 2003.

Larsen, Michael. *How to Get a Literary Agent.* Naperville, IL: Sourcebooks, 2006.

Leder, Meg, and Jack Heffron, eds. *The Complete Handbook of Novel Writing.* Cincinnati: Writers Digest Books, 2002.

Sands, Katherine, ed. *Making the Perfect Pitch: Advice from 45 Top Book Agents.* Waukesha, WI: Kalmbach Publishing, 2004.

Thiel, Diane. *Open Roads: Exercises in Writing Poetry.* Boston: Longman, 2004.

NONFICTION

Gerard, Philip, and Carolyn Forche, eds. *Writing Creative Nonfiction: Instruction and Insights from Teachers of the Associated Writing Programs.* Cincinnati: Writers Digest Books, 2001.

Poynter, Dan. *Writing Nonfiction: Turning Thoughts into Books*, 4th ed. Santa Barbara, CA: Para Publishing, 2005.

FREELANCE, MAGAZINES, AND NEWSPAPERS

Bly, Robert W. *Getting Started as a Freelance Writer.* Boulder, CO: Sentient Publications, 2006.

Dick, Jill. *Freelance Writing for Newspapers*, 3rd ed. London: A & C Black, 2003.

Trottier, David. *The Freelance Writer's Bible: Your Guide to a Profitable Writing Career Within One Year*. Los Angeles: Silman-James Press, 2006.

Wisniski, Joe. *Writing for Publication—A Step-by-Step Guide to Making Money by Writing for Newspapers and Magazines*. Lulu.com, 2004.

SCREENWRITING

Field, Syd. *Screenplay: The Foundations of Screenwriting*. El Dorado, AR: Delta Press, 2005.

Henson, Wendy J. *Screenwriting: Step by Step*. Boston: Allyn & Bacon, 2004.

Suppa, Ron. *Real Screenwriting: Strategies and Stories from the Trenches*. Florence, KY: Course Technology PTR, 2005.

TECHNICAL WRITING

Holloway, Brian R. *Technical Writing Basics: A Guide to Style and Form*, 3rd ed. Upper Saddle River, NJ: Prentice Hall, 2004.

Pringle, Alan S., and Sarah S. O'Keefe. *Technical Writing 101: A Real-World Guide to Planing and Writing Technical Documentation*, 2nd ed. Research Triangle Park, NC: Scriptorium Press, 2003.

MARKETING, ADVERTISING, AND PUBLIC RELATIONS

Camenson, Blythe, *Great Jobs for Communications Majors*, 2nd ed. New York: McGraw-Hill, 2001.

Davis, Kenneth W. *The McGraw-Hill 36-Hour Course in Business Writing and Communication*. New York: McGraw-Hill, 2005.

Higgins, Dennis. *The Art of Writing Advertising: Conversations with Masters of the Craft: David Ogilvy, William Bernbach, Leo Burnett, Rosser Reeves*. New York: McGraw-Hill, 2003.

Marsh, Charles, et al. *Strategic Writing: Multimedia Writing for Public Relations, Advertising, Sales and Marketing, and Business Communication*. Boston: Allyn & Bacon, 2004.

National Register, ed. *Standard Directory of Advertising Agencies.* New Providence, NJ: National Register Publishing, 2003.

Wilcox, Dennis L. *Public Relations Writing and Media Techniques*, 5th ed. Boston, Allyn & Bacon, 2005.

MARKET GUIDES

Council of Literary Press and Magazines. *The Literary Press and Magazine Directory 2006/2007: The Only Directory for the Serious Writer of Fiction and Poetry*. Brooklyn, NY: Soft Skull Press, 2006.

Fulton, Len. *The International Directory of Little Magazines and Small Presses 2006/2007*. Paradise, CA: Dustbooks, 2006.

The following guides are all available from Writers Digest Books. Visit www.writersdigest.com for information.

Artist's and Graphic Designer's Market
Children's Writer's and Illustrator's Market
Guide to Literary Agents
Novel and Short Story Writer's Market
Photographer's Market
Poet's Market
Writer's Market
Writer's Online Marketplace

ABOUT THE AUTHOR

Blythe Camenson is a full-time writer with more than four dozen books and numerous articles to her credit, including *Your Novel Proposal: From Creation to Contract* (Writer's Digest Books), which she coauthored with Marshall J. Cook.

As director of Fiction Writer's Connection (fictionwriters.com), a membership organization for new writers, she edits and writes for *Fiction Writer's Guideline* (the FWC newsletter), provides a free critiquing service to members, teaches e-mail courses on how to write and get published, and speaks at various writers' conferences and workshops.